"Friendly, passionate, intellectual, and ( and contemporary affairs, Francis Scha( tionate portrait. Rescued from the disto. ........ ......... demonizers, here is Schaeffer as so many of us knew him in the great years of L'Abri—and with so much to contribute to our world today."

**Os Guinness,** author, *A Free People's Suicide*

"An engaging, fascinating account, seasoned with unusual insight into one of the truly original apologists of our time."

**David F. Wells,** Distinguished Research Professor, Gordon-Conwell Theological Seminary

"For many years I hoped that I could spend some time at L'Abri, but that was not God's plan for me. Instead, God enabled me to become friends with many L'Abri alumni, of whom Bill Edgar is one. I have been impressed with the intellectual caliber of those men and women, but even more with their godly character. L'Abri evidently had a way of leading people from intellectual atheism, to conversion, to spiritual maturity. Bill's book focuses, more than other L'Abri books, on this process of what we now call spiritual formation. The whole church can learn much from it. I commend this excellent book to all who seek to draw nearer to God."

**John M. Frame,** J. D. Trimble Chair of Systematic Theology and Philosophy, Reformed Theological Seminary, Orlando

"Francis Schaeffer was small of stature but a giant in his tenacious concern for truth, for God, for people, and for reality. He became convinced that Christian faith is the radical path for our own day, the realistic answer to the hard questions of a troubled modern world. William Edgar's compulsively readable study of Schaeffer's thought is set in the context of Schaeffer's rough-edged life and his brilliantly inspired work in the L'Abri community he established with his remarkable wife, Edith. L'Abri, perched high on the slopes of a remote alpine valley, drew a motley procession of mainly young travelers from the ends of the earth. Schaeffer's own, sometimes anguished, quest to communicate the ancient biblical text in a century of unprecedented historical changes attracted and opened doors for a generation of Christians. It also convinced many outside the faith with honest questions (like Bill Edgar himself) to follow the way of Christ. This engaging book captures the fire of Francis Schaeffer's thought and concerns, and revisits and reinvigorates the still-urgent challenge he presented to the church in the modern world."

**Colin Duriez,** author, *Francis Schaeffer: An Authentic Life*

"Dr. Edgar's book on countercultural spirituality is a much-needed and trustworthy guide in the dark confusion of the postmodern world."

**Wim G. Rietkerk,** Trustee, L'Abri Fellowship, Holland

"In a brilliant combination of personal recollections and thorough analysis, William Edgar demonstrates convincingly that the Schaeffers' encounter with the triune God who is there is central to the rise, growth, and impact of L'Abri. This refreshing study will arouse the enthusiasm of all who yearn for a true spirituality that transforms minds and lives, regenerates the church, and 'flows into the total culture.'"

**Pierre Berthoud,** Professor Emeritus, Faculté Jean Calvin, Aix-en Provence

# SCHAEFFER

*on the Christian Life*

# THEOLOGIANS ON THE CHRISTIAN LIFE

## A SERIES

### EDITED BY STEPHEN J. NICHOLS AND JUSTIN TAYLOR

# SCHAEFFER

*on the Christian Life*

## COUNTERCULTURAL SPIRITUALITY

## WILLIAM EDGAR

WHEATON, ILLINOIS

*Schaeffer on the Christian Life: Countercultural Spirituality*

Copyright © 2013 by William Edgar

Published by Crossway
    1300 Crescent Street
    Wheaton, Illinois 60187

Cover design: Josh Dennis

Cover image: Richard Solomon Artists, Mark Summers

First printing 2013

Printed in the United States of America

The author's Scripture quotations are from the ESV® Bible (*The Holy Bible, English Standard Version®*), copyright © 2001 by Crossway. 2011 Text Edition. Used by permission. All rights reserved.

Trade paperback ISBN: 978-1-4335-3139-2
PDF ISBN: 978-1-4335-3140-8
Mobipocket ISBN: 978-1-4335-3141-5
ePub ISBN: 978-1-4335-3142-2

**Library of Congress Cataloging-in-Publication Data**

Edgar, William, 1944–
    Schaeffer on the Christian life : countercultural spirituality / William Edgar.
        p. cm.—(Theologians on the Christian life)
    Includes bibliographical references and index.
    ISBN 978-1-4335-3139-2
    1. Schaeffer, Francis A. (Francis August) 2. Evangelicalism. 3. Christian life. I. Title.
    BR1643.S33E34        2013
    248.4—dc23                        2012031495

Crossway is a publishing ministry of Good News Publishers.

| VP | | 22 | 21 | 20 | 19 | 18 | 17 | 16 | 15 | 14 | 13 |
|----|----|----|----|----|----|----|----|----|----|----|----|
| 15 | 14 | 13 | 12 | 11 | 10 | 9 | 8 | 7 | 6 | 5 | 4 | 3 | 2 | 1 |

*To Dick and Mardi Keyes,*
*who embody the spirit of L'Abri*
*for our generation*

# CONTENTS

# SERIES PREFACE

Some might call us spoiled. We live in an era of significant and substantial resources for Christians on living the Christian life. We have ready access to books, DVD series, online material, seminars—all in the interest of encouraging us in our daily walk with Christ. The laity, the people in the pew, have access to more information than scholars dreamed of having in previous centuries.

Yet for all our abundance of resources, we also lack something. We tend to lack the perspectives from the past, perspectives from a different time and place than our own. To put the matter differently, we have so many riches in our current horizon that we tend not to look to the horizons of the past.

That is unfortunate, especially when it comes to learning about and practicing discipleship. It's like owning a mansion and choosing to live in only one room. This series invites you to explore the other rooms.

As we go exploring, we will visit places and times different from our own. We will see different models, approaches, and emphases. This series does not intend for these models to be copied uncritically, and it certainly does not intend to put these figures from the past high upon a pedestal like some race of super-Christians. This series intends, however, to help us in the present listen to the past. We believe there is wisdom in the past twenty centuries of the church, wisdom for living the Christian life.

Stephen J. Nichols and Justin Taylor

# PREFACE

When I was first approached to write this book, I declined. There have been a number of significant biographies of Francis Schaeffer, as well as a thorough accounting of his family's life and times by Edith Schaeffer. Much of this material is thoughtful, though some of it is merely hagiographical, and some of it unjustly critical. To be sure, I have my own take on this extraordinary ministry and its astonishing founder. Indeed, it is because of L'Abri that my own eyes were opened to the beauties of the Christian faith many years ago. But it seemed to me that there was plenty of material and that one more study would be extraneous. Besides, opinions run strong, even this many years after Dr. Schaeffer's departure from this earth, and my temperament is sensitive, making me particularly susceptible to the inevitable criticisms such a book would receive.

A couple of things changed my mind. The first is that despite all of the analysis already done on Francis Schaeffer and the work of L'Abri, very little has been said in any kind of depth about their most significant *raison d'être*, that is, Christian spirituality. There is a need for a careful study of the subject Schaeffer himself considered central to all his work. Second, I began to think how important to my own thinking and self-evaluation such a study could be now nearly fifty years after my initial encounter with the man. Not, I trust, a thinly veiled attempt at self-discovery, which would be not only narcissistic but also of little benefit to the reading public, the present exploration has afforded me the opportunity to think through issues that matter greatly to the church and the world. No doubt I could have accomplished that without publishing a book on the subject, but there is something about getting words on a page, and then receiving peer review, that can help make such a task more than personal musings, edifying or not. Third, I have always been grateful to Crossway for their vision, especially their desire to promote the work of L'Abri and the thought of Francis and Edith Schaeffer. Writing this book gives me the chance to respond in gratitude to that vision and possibly to make a small contribution to its goals.

The format of this volume needs a word of explanation. Because I was privileged personally to witness many of the themes and personalities connected with Francis Schaeffer and L'Abri, I have begun and ended with some narrative involving my own story. Thus, the first chapter is a personal introduction explaining the way in which I saw Francis Schaeffer "up close and personal." In the afterword I offer a few concluding personal reflections. They are not meant to distract from the analytical portions of the book, but to make them more personable. I trust the reader will enjoy these reflections rather than be put off by them.

Is Francis Schaeffer in the same league as Saint Augustine, Martin Luther, John Calvin, John Wesley, Dietrich Bonhoeffer, and the other figures in the Theologians on the Christian Life series? Had you asked me twenty years ago, I would have said no. It would be hard to overstate my love for the man. However, I thought he had neither the academic standing nor perhaps the influence wielded by these giants. His writings and films often seemed dated, and his principal legacy is no doubt people, not a movement based on revolutionary ideas. I was always a bit troubled by comparisons made between him and C. S. Lewis, whose stature is nothing if not towering. But today I gladly agree that Schaeffer belongs to this hall of fame.

A legacy of people is just the reason why. Schaeffer's importance is because of the way he could take God, thinkers, and truth and make them so profoundly exciting—to people! Os Guinness, one of Schaeffer's closest associates, tells us he has never met anyone like him anywhere "who took God so passionately seriously, people so passionately seriously, and truth so passionately seriously."[1] While a number of Schaeffer's ideas or historical assessments could and should be put into question, what is unquestionable is the way Francis Schaeffer moved from the heart of the Christian faith, or "true spirituality," into every realm of life, with absolute continuity and astonishing freshness, and communicated all of that to so many people. I am honored to be asked to help defend such a legacy.

[1] Os Guinness, "Fathers and Sons," *Books and Culture* 14, no. 2 (March/April 2008): 33.

One challenge that presents itself in discussions of a figure such as Francis Schaeffer is that he was not typically speaking as a systematic theologian in an academic setting. Like many thinkers and spokespersons called "for such a time as this" (Est. 4:14), he responded to his generation with those portions of the truth he deemed most needful. Although he was committed to preaching "the whole counsel of God" (Acts 20:27), he naturally did not spend an equal amount of time on every locus of theology. If you are looking for an extended treatment of, say, the nature of the covenant or the ethics of marriage and divorce, you should probably look elsewhere. Schaeffer had his views on such subjects and indeed knew the big picture, as his series on the Westminster Standards will attest, but the balance of his work was on apologetics, cultural analysis, the defense of the Bible, and the like.

Thus, some of what you read in these pages may seem one-sided. Most frequently, though, that is not because Schaeffer was unbalanced, but because he was acutely aware that to respond to all kinds of issues but not the most urgent ones is to fail to herald the gospel at that point. Schaeffer often quoted a saying attributed to Martin Luther, but in fact spoken by the character "Fritz" in a historical novel, whose voice supports Luther's ideas: "If I profess, with the loudest voice and the clearest exposition, every portion of the truth of God except precisely that little point which the world and the devil are at that moment attacking, I am not confessing Christ, however boldly I may be professing Christianity."[2] Schaeffer also used to say fairly regularly that his own writings were only one aspect of the work of L'Abri. If one wanted to obtain a full grasp of the overall message, one needed to consult not only Edith's books, but also his sermons and lecture series. This I have endeavored to do.

I wish here to express my thanks to a number of people and institutions that have given me much-needed though ill-deserved support throughout the writing of this book. First, I thank my kind and generous editors at Crossway for their inspiration and also their meticulous editing work. They represent the gold standard.

Second, I would like to express my thanks to three people who have brought particular insight to this project. The first is my wife, Barbara, who not only caught a number of infelicities but also made helpful editorial comments. She also sacrificed our dining room table for the better part

---

[2] Elizabeth Rundle Charles, *Chronicles of the Schönberg-Cotta Family* (New York: Thomas Nelson, 1864), 276.

of four months so that I could spread all my sources out for easy access. The second is Colin Duriez, Schaeffer's biographer, who not only has been most encouraging to me but also made a number of very helpful editorial comments.

Third, I am very grateful to Jerram Barrs, whose wise and pointed comments made this a much better book than it might have been. Finally, thanks are due to Westminster Theological Seminary, which was kind enough to rearrange my schedule so that I could have blocks of time in which to work on this text. The president, the dean, my dear colleagues, and the staff of the seminary have supported me in my lifelong attempts at saying no to the urgent, and yes to the vital.

William Edgar
Philadelphia

# CHAPTER I

# A PERSONAL INTRODUCTION TO FRANCIS SCHAEFFER

*Schaeffer might be dismissed as a scholar or even original thinker (though it can be argued he was both, but particularly the latter), but his realistic, existential Christianity is remarkable and perhaps unique for someone of his biblical orthodoxy in his generation and is the secret, perhaps, of his impact on many people of diverse backgrounds and nationalities.*

COLIN DURIEZ

### First Impressions

I hopped off the mail bus on a warm afternoon in July 1964, having asked the driver, "Arrêtez-vous, s'il vous plaît, à L'Abri." The name L'Abri means "The Shelter," and it was first coined by Francis Schaeffer in Champéry, the village in Switzerland where the family had lived before relocating to Huémoz-sur-Ollon, a tiny village in the Protestant canton de Vaud. The name is based on Psalm 91:1:

> He who dwells in the shelter of the Most High
>   will abide in the shadow of the Almighty.

I was unaware of any of the history of this magical place, arriving at the Schaeffers' door as a rising college junior, aged nineteen.

My whole life was about to change. I was not a believer at the time and so was unaware of many of the claims for the Christian view of the world. Yet, thanks to a man named Joe Brown, I had become intrigued and was open to hearing about spiritual matters in a way I had never been before. A marvelous instructor at Harvard College, Harold O. J. Brown (1933–2007), presented the glories of the Christian faith to his classes during the academic year 1963–1964. By the spring Joe and I had become good friends. He saw that I was spiritually hungry, and he urged me to visit his friend Francis Schaeffer over the summer, in the hopes that I could learn more about the same worldview that he had labored to commend in his lectures. Indeed, as I would soon learn, he really sent me there in the hopes that I could embrace the Christian faith.

Joe was a teaching assistant for a large course in the history of Western epic and drama, known affectionately as "Hum 2" by the students. The main lecturer was the legendary John Finley, crafter of America's postwar general education approach to university studies. As an article about him in the *Harvard Crimson* put it, in appearance he combined the best traits of Henry James's English gentleman and Robert Frost's New England farmer.[1] His concern was that a person was not truly educated if he became so specialized that he lost sight of the big picture, including issues such as meaning, fulfillment, and human flourishing. This meant students had to be much more aware than they typically were of Western history and traditional humanistic values.

Hum 2 was a large class, and so for practical reasons it was broken down into smaller groups, called sections. Here students could have a more personalized access to the material. Our section instructor was Joe, who was working in the History Department of the graduate school, writing his dissertation on Laski (Johannes Alasco), the Polish reformer of the sixteenth century. Joe was unabashed (though tactful), even brilliant, in his presentation of evangelical Christianity in contrast to various worldviews held by the ancient Greeks or the modern absurdists. All of it was new and immensely fascinating to me, a young man in my late teens. Joe and I became friends and had many long conversations about matters of faith and life.

So, on the strength of Joe's recommendation, as I traveled through

---

[1] John D. Reed, "John Finley: Profile," *Harvard Crimson*, February 21, 1967, available at http://www.thecrimson.com/article/1967/2/21/john-finley-ponce-upon-a-time/.

Europe with my brother and a backpack full of essentials, I looked for a chance to check out Francis Schaeffer. In mid-July my brother returned to the States. Now on my own, I took the train down from Zürich, where we had been visiting a colleague of our dad's, to the beautiful city of Lausanne, on the shore of Lake Geneva. I had called in advance and got Mrs. Schaeffer on the phone. She could not have been more welcoming and said that Joe Brown was their good friend. He had no doubt alerted them to my possible visit. She invited me to stay for the weekend, which was a bit curious to me but very agreeable.

The day was Saturday, and I had some time to kill, so on the way to L'Abri I visited the Lausanne Expo 1964, a fascinating display of technology and economic opportunities, couched in the culture of the Cold War. The Swiss architect Marc Saugey had the idea of using large tents for a major part of the Lausanne exhibition. They were meant to symbolize the Swiss Alps with their snow and rocks. They involved membrane structures swinging about and housing artistic and futuristic technological offerings.[2]

After the visit to the expo, I caught the train over to Aigle, a sprawling town at the foot of the Chablais Alps, just beyond the lake to the east. Then, I switched to a cog railroad train up the steep mountain to the small town of Ollon. Perfectly timed, the mail bus then stopped at the station to pick up passengers on their way to Villars, a lovely ski town at the very summit. Huémoz, a tiny village situated at 2,160 feet above sea level, is about halfway to Villars. On the bus's steering wheel was a knob, used by the driver to swing his way around and up the considerably winding road with no shoulders, as he somehow managed to avoid tumbling down the precipitous hills below. The air was pure and the weather temperate, even in the middle of the summer. A couple of other students headed for L'Abri were on the bus with me. Anticipation and some nervousness inhabited my youthful soul. But these were the 1960s. I was on a most excellent adventure!

It was all quite astonishing. At the stop in Huémoz we were greeted by Coxie Priester, Dr. Schaeffer's secretary, who remains my good friend to this day. Right away Coxie asked whether I was a Christian. I wasn't sure, so I told her the question was ambiguous. With a twinkle she remarked that the answer was ambiguous, not the question. I would soon find out

---

[2] All this was significant in that the contents of this fair would be the subject of discussion at L'Abri. The whole display was deemed "humanistic," a negative label (unlike what I was used to) that I would hear often in the following weeks.

how right she was. I walked up the stairs to the main house, "Les Mélèzes," a magnificent old-fashioned Swiss chalet, lined, as the name suggested, with timberline larches. The building boasted two large balconies, several bedrooms, a spacious living room downstairs, and a small but functional kitchen. I was invited to enter the living room, where we were to help prepare Sunday's dinner. A young woman handed me a brown bag filled with peas in their pods, and asked if I could help remove them. The procedure took a while, as we would be feeding at least forty people. But the time passed easily because our hosts played a tape for us while we worked.

Some readers may remember the reel-to-reel tape machines we had back then. There was loud clicking whenever a section was replayed. In this case the lecturer sounded like a highly qualified woman, who was expounding on existentialism. This was a good test for me of L'Abri's authenticity, as I had actually read a good deal in this philosophy and indeed fancied myself an existentialist in the tradition of my hero, Albert Camus. Having grown up in France in the 1950s, I had gravitated toward this prophet of the absurd and was fairly convinced of his approach to life and to human justice. The speaker carefully contrasted Camus with Jean-Paul Sartre and rather impressed me with her knowledge. I had been wary of Sartre's darker approach to life and was glad to hear the lecturer side with Camus. Then she brought in the "religious" existentialists. I cannot remember which names were used. For me the outstanding exponent of religious existentialism was Paul Claudel, the Roman Catholic playwright and philosopher. However, the speaker was most concerned with Søren Kierkegaard, which she pronounced "Kerkigard" and dubbed the father of modern existentialism. I was less sure about this attribution but listened on.

Boiling it down, the Danish theologian's views were summarized as an invitation to an irrational "leap of faith."[3] That was the basis for everything that followed, much of which was a quite negative description of

---

[3] Somewhat later Schaeffer would temper his view by recognizing that the more existentialist interpretation of Kierkegaard may have come from his followers' applications rather than the man himself (see *The Church at the End of the Twentieth Century* [Downers Grove, IL: InterVarsity, 1970], 17). In the *Complete Works* the reference is 4:14. Throughout this volume I generally will refer to *The Complete Works of Francis A. Schaeffer* (Westchester, IL: Crossway, 1982), hereafter *CW*, which unites all of his major writings except *The Great Evangelical Disaster*, published in 1984, and smaller essays and booklets such as *Baptism*. The *Complete Works* are in five volumes, which I will cite by volume number followed by the page number. (For a list of titles in the *Complete Works* by volume numbers, see the appendix.) An advantage to citing this set is that Schaeffer was able to edit or update a number of the texts. Occasionally I will refer also to an original edition, particularly when the date of publication or the unedited original is significant.

the current intellectual climate. The lecturer went on to discuss a larger consideration of what was called "the existentialist methodology," an approach embraced by both philosophers and theologians. Life in this view was dichotomized between a "lower story" and an "upper story," so that matters of faith were thought to be beyond reason's reach. I was deeply impressed, though I could hardly grasp it all.

Strangely, it turned out that the lecturer was none other than Francis Schaeffer! He did have a rather high-pitched voice, but the recording made him sound quite like a woman. The content was riveting. Not only the linear analysis of trends leading to existentialism and beyond, but the vivid illustrations too were captivating.

After the peas were all removed from their pods, I went outside. Along came the man himself. I knew right away who he was, even though I had never seen a picture of him. His face was radiant. Slightly wrinkled, his visage communicated the weight of many years, years of suffering and of pondering deeply, and yet also a fundamental joy. He was fifty-two at the time. He came right up to me, obviously knowing who I was, and extended his hand for a warm greeting. I'll never forget his broad smile, so full of kindness. He was genuinely glad to see me. I felt right at home in this strange and wonderful place. Joe had not prepared me for any of this, probably wisely so. But I couldn't wait to get to know Dr. Schaeffer better and find out what the magic was.

That evening we had a cookout—American hot dogs. There I met some remarkable people, mostly non-Americans. They were at various stages of religious understanding, some from a Christian background, but many of them "seekers" (as we would later call them). One of my new friends was Jonathan Bragdon, Edith's nephew, who was at L'Abri out of curiosity for what this branch of the family had created. His mother had become a Taylorite, part of the extremist wing of the Plymouth Brethren. It called for radical separation from anyone who held to the slightest variant of the true faith. Mrs. Bragdon had even "disfellowshiped" her own husband. Needless to say, this view was not working for Jonathan. He was, and is, a practicing painter. He was quite taken with Paul Klee (1879–1940), someone whose work I loved very much. Since I was studying music at Harvard and had a strong interest in aesthetics, we enjoyed extended conversations about the arts. I had never thought of this subject from a Christian point of view, but soon would be regularly connecting faith to the arts.

After the meal, following cleanup, we went into the living room for the Saturday night discussion group. In fact, "discussion" meant someone would ask a question, and then Dr. Schaeffer would answer it, often taking a good long time to construct his response. We all arrived a bit weary from the day's adventures and sat cross-legged on the floor; then after a bit of a wait, Fran walked in.[4] He greeted various ones, then sat down on a quaint little red stool Edith had made from a barrel, and opened with, "Yes, then, who would like to begin?" He almost always began his discourses with "yes, then," or "well, then," followed by the subject at hand. That night, most of the discussion revolved around the subject of prayer.

I had never heard anything remotely like this. The only prayers I knew about were from the Episcopal liturgy said every day in my boarding-school chapel services. Most of us chapel attendees either did not listen or pretended not to listen. In point of fact, those prayers were actually embedded in my psyche somewhere, so that when I did come to faith, they came up to the surface and, I am sure, helped me progress more rapidly than if I had never heard them. Here at L'Abri, prayer was not a ritual. It was utterly real. Prayer was practiced as though, were there no God, this would have been the most absurd performance possible. Schaeffer continued for a good long time, explaining that when we prayed, God heard. Indeed, God perfected our "poor prayers" and made them acceptable to himself. Then God would answer. Sometimes the answer was affirmative, giving us what we had asked. Often, though, the answer was in a different direction from what we had intended, but always for our greater good.

Schaeffer gave some moving examples about the effectiveness of prayer. For instance, on an airplane trip he took to the States, two engines on the same wing failed. The plane descended rapidly until it was just about to crash into the waves, when suddenly the power came back on. Schaeffer had been praying, he explained. So had his family back home, having heard a newsflash on the radio about a struggling plane. There was a sort of prayer triangle, he argued—plane-to-God, home-to-God, and then the answer, God-to-plane. On the way out, Schaeffer greeted the astonished pilot, who could find no reason for the sudden reigniting. "Prayer," Fran affirmed confidently. Of course, I did not absorb or fully understand all of this. It was all too new and quite exotic for me. I would later understand

[4] The gentle reader will forgive me if I occasionally call them Fran and Edith, as I did through the years. Though thirty years my elders, they became such close friends that I was comfortable with them on a first-name basis.

that the Holy Spirit was prompting me, moving me toward the Savior. But for now, it was simply something from another world.

After the long evening of discussion on prayer as well as a few other topics, someone was asked to close in prayer. A sleepy-eyed student came to and uttered some sort of parting words of thanksgiving. Then Schaeffer got up, headed straight my way, and said something a bit strange, but which made perfect sense in retrospect. He told me he was not preaching the next day, so he would not be completely exhausted after the morning worship. He could therefore spend some time with me before lunch. Please, could I think of a key question I needed to ask concerning the faith when I came for this visit? I went to bed cogitating on what my question might be. I am somewhat ashamed to say it was a sophisticated-sounding version of *so what?* I think my formulation was something like this: what is the relevance of this Christian faith, even if it could be proved to be true?

The next day we held a church service. Again, I had never experienced anything like this. Chairs were brought in to the Les Mélèzes living room, where we had enjoyed the discussion the night before. We sat there and, after some opening words, began to sing Bach chorales in four-part harmony. How good could it get? As a music student, I had spent two years at Harvard analyzing Bach. Indeed, a thorough knowledge of these chorales was a prerequisite for our theory courses. And here we were, not studying them but singing them, and believing them. Then came the message. Ranald Macaulay, today my dear friend, preached in his kilt, the Macaulay tartan. It was a stirring sermon about reconciling Paul and James on their apparent differences over the relation of justification and good works. Rather than withdrawing or cynically thinking, *so glad he's excited about this*, I tried to enter into the issue and the arguments. Over an hour later, Ranald appeared to have concluded, and he certainly convinced me, even though I did not know much about what was involved. Only later, in theological seminary, would I be introduced at the scholarly level to the conundrum about the book of James's rhetorical arguments concerning salvation by good works. My professors confirmed that Paul and James were on the same page. But I already knew this, through Ranald!

So then the moment arrived. I made my way upstairs to the little chamber outside the bedrooms where Francis Schaeffer liked to counsel people. With that same profound face, its warm grin, and the clear sense that he really cared about me as well as the issues we needed to discuss, he asked whether I had thought of my question. I spouted out my question about relevance, and he came back with an extensive, thoughtful reply. His answer included the "free-will defense" for the problem of evil, and the importance of human significance, owing to our being made after God's image. We went back and forth. After a couple of hours, I just knew this was all true. If it is possible to *feel* the Holy Spirit come into one's heart, I could, and I did. I was a Christian!

Fran then directed me to pray, which I had never done, at least in any sort of personal manner. What should I say, I asked? Just "thank you" will do very nicely, he replied. So, my face bathed in tears, I thanked the good Lord for leading me into his family. Fran frequently accompanied my phrases with groans of agreement, which I would later learn is a standard evangelical way of praying together. He then prayed for me, and we prayed together for Joe and for many other things we seemed to care about mutually.

Less than twenty-four hours after my arrival at L'Abri my life was completely turned upside down. Or was it right side up? I went down to the marvelous Sunday lunch, complete with my fresh peas, served outside on a large table that could fit at least thirty people. A rather long grace was said. I would have to get used to smelling the excellent savors of the great cooking at L'Abri while the praying person went from Genesis to Revelation, then the cosmos, then the rich and the poor, and so on. During the meal, more wonderful conversation ensued. Most of us who frequented L'Abri in those days would likely affirm that we learned more around the table, or during the walks afterward, than in the official seminars, good as they were. I decided I desperately needed to stay here longer. I asked Fran if that were possible. Well, he said, they were unusually crowded: thirty-five students plus staff. But he would see what he could do. Little did any of us know that a few years later the Vaudois government would have to put a cap on the community at 130 people!

### A Mentor and a Friend

In the midst of all of this, I received a phone call from my dad, telling me some astonishing news. His company had moved him to Geneva. This meant I would be freer to come and go to L'Abri, a great personal encouragement. At any rate, after a brief trip apartment-hunting with Dad, I did return to L'Abri and stayed out the summer. Fran urged me to listen to his Romans series, some verse-by-verse Bible studies on Romans 1–8, given in a Lausanne café, complete with the sounds of dishes served and customers ordering food.[5] He also wanted me to listen to some lectures entitled "The Intellectual Climate and the New Theology." If there was time, I was to go on to cover the "Basic Christian Doctrines" series, a study of the Westminster Confession of Faith. I did all these and was thoroughly stirred by the extraordinary content, radically fresh to this new believer.

In later years I would return to L'Abri over and over, as often as my study and work schedule permitted me. I became so conversant with the message and the life there that I used to play a game with myself: could I predict the next words to come out of Fran's mouth? Most of the time I could, but not always. He always stayed fresh!

These first impressions of Francis Schaeffer, I would discover, were from the fruit of the strange and wonderful history of L'Abri. Much of it flowed from the Schaeffers' views on spirituality, which in turn fed into their apologetics. The Schaeffers were strongly driven by a sense of mission. The mission was hammered out on the anvil of experience. The historical background will be more fully explained in the next chapters. The purpose of L'Abri was to welcome people and introduce them to the gospel. What they set forth to anyone who would come and listen was not only the explanation of the way into heaven, though that was tantamount, but the application of the Christian worldview to all of life. The warm welcome was genuine. Indeed, it resulted from a prayer that was often said at L'Abri: "Lord, bring us the people of your choice." While sounding like a tautology (who else would the Lord bring?), what this prayer signified in practice was that whoever showed up at L'Abri was meant to be there by divine providence. And thus every guest was treated as though he or she were a special envoy. The extraordinary combination of community life and intellectual challenge was essential to the fabric of life in Huémoz.

Francis Schaeffer was a brilliant man. His method of learning was less the careful study of textbooks with footnotes and more an informal collecting of insights from Scripture, people, articles, clippings, and his own hunches. He had a "nose" for generalizations. Occasionally they were oversimple or even mistaken. But mostly he had a sense of what was reasonable and what was not, and would explore his ideas accordingly. He

---

[5] These studies were later transcribed, edited, and published as *The Finished Work of Christ: The Truth of Romans 1–8* (Wheaton, IL: Crossway, 1998).

possessed a considerable knowledge of the arts and was able to converse about them or most any other subject with just about anybody who would come across his path.

I once sent him some material about John Cage, the radical American avant-garde composer. It came from one of the *New Yorker* "Profiles," and was a rather long article based on interviews.[6] Cage was an *enfant terrible*. He wrote such disturbing pieces as *4'33"*, the score of which calls for the musician "not to play the notes," resulting in four minutes and thirty-three seconds of silence. He composed *Imaginary Landscape No. 4*, a performance in which twelve radios were played at once. He claimed he was a Zen Buddhist, believing the universe to be based on chance and "purposeless play." Schaeffer saw something in the profile that I had not. As was well known, Cage had a special avocation: mycology (the study of fungi, especially mushrooms). After exploring this field, the interviewer asked Cage how he could reconcile his orderly mushroom collections with a chance universe. Oh, said Cage, if I had to collect mushrooms on the basis of my Zen convictions I would surely die. Fran often used this as an example of the impossibility of a worldview that tried consistently to deny the inherent order of God's universe. It simply couldn't "fit" into reality.

In addition to my regular visits to L'Abri, among the many ways my friendship with Francis Schaeffer would develop over the years were several occasions when he came to America. While I was still at Harvard, Joe Brown led a few of us to invite Schaeffer to give some lectures at the university about the basics of Christian apologetics. They were to be called the CCTL, the Christian Contemporary Thought Lectures. The series would eventually include Herman Dooyeweerd (1894–1977) and Georges Florovsky (1893–1979). Funded by a friend from Park Street Church in Boston, these lectures were given in Lowell Lecture Hall.

When Schaeffer came, the place was packed. Nothing quite like it had ever been heard at Harvard, I am fairly certain. He appeared in his typical Swiss hiking outfit.[7] He spoke in his high-pitched voice about the "line of despair," frequently drawing on the blackboard behind him. He threw out names: Hegel, Kierkegaard, Freud, Sartre, Camus, and many others. But what was most memorable was his passionate appeal for *consistency*.

---

[6] Calvin Tomkins, "Figure in an Imaginary Landscape," *The New Yorker*, November 28, 1964, 64–128.
[7] Schaeffer's dress code is a matter of some curiosity. In later years he wore a Nehru jacket and hiking shoes, grew his hair long, and sported a goatee. Cynics thought it was a way of getting attention. My own view is that it was part of an overall statement about the radical nature of the true biblical message. True Christianity for him was revolutionary and nonconformist—and he had the clothes to match!

These philosophers were unable to articulate a point of view that in the end could account for the world around them. A lack of such consistency was, again, for Schaeffer evidence of the impossibility of succeeding in God's world without a biblical view of life.

He told us of a man he once met on shipboard. The fellow found out Fran was a pastor and immediately decided to have some fun (as a classmate sitting next to me in the lecture whispered into my ear: not a great idea!). The man had claimed that there was no real meaning in life and no way to access truth. Pastors were naïve people living in an idealistic world. For the man, life had no meaning and nothing was real. Schaeffer asked him bluntly whether when he would go below and embrace his wife, he would have any assurance that she was really there! The man was furious and left with a short riposte, "Of course I know she is there," but he was clearly caught off guard and embarrassed. The riveted audience began to have a sense that a real, meaningful life without acknowledging the God of the universe was neither possible nor desirable.[8]

Most of my friends at Harvard were skeptics or even atheists. I had become a Christian rather dramatically, to their astonishment. These friends remained cordial and even affectionate, but they clearly thought I had gone a bit wacky, whereas I used to be so normal. They wondered about this "guru" I had met. So on the occasion of one of the CCTL lectures I invited a dozen of them to meet Fran in the private dining room in Kirkland House, my place of residence. As the time approached, I grew rather nervous. My friends were brilliant, budding leaders in their fields. I began to worry that my guru would be out of his depth. He arrived a bit late because he had been engaged in a conversation. I rather awkwardly introduced him as someone who believed in truth and that the Bible had basic answers for all of life. As the discussion moved forward I felt somewhat better.

Then came two questions from two of my best friends. The first was about whether Theravada or Mahayana Buddhists were the authentic successors of Siddartha's thought. Oh dear, I thought, he doesn't know the first thing about these finer points of world religions. To my surprise and delight he replied that three thousand years before the Christian era,

---

[8] Cornelius Van Til (1895–1987), Schaeffer's professor at Westminster Seminary, used to refer to the "presuppositional" method of validating the Christian faith as the "impossibility of the contrary." See his *Defense of the Faith*, 3rd ed. (Nutley, NJ: Presbyterian and Reformed, 1967), 100–101. I shall make further comments on this idea below.

tradesmen had crossed paths in the Indus valley and as a result of their exchanging ideas about the gods, they had produced a synthesis resulting in the impersonal, pantheistic worldview of Eastern religion. Therefore, in the Asian perspective, we cannot deal with evil as a reality. I was bowled over. I later found out someone had sent him an article about this, and he had stored up the information in a mental file somewhere!

A second question came that I was sure would undo him. One of my close friends was on the cutting edge of urban planning. The computer was in its very early stages, and he thought that we could solve many problems in our cities through the computer and other calculating machines. Again, I thought, Dr. Schaeffer has no idea what is going on in this field. And again, he came right back: but what about the place of the human being in all this? My friend, along with the rest in the room, was stunned. It's all about anthropology, Schaeffer explained. At the end of the time, they all flocked to him for follow up. One of my dearest friends in the room was an African American in premedical studies.[9] The two of us had many interests in common, including jazz music and theology. He had written a fascinating paper on philosophy and handed it to Schaeffer hoping for an evaluation. Others followed. Schaeffer once told me he loved receiving these papers but found it nearly impossible to read them carefully and give thoughtful answers to them. But he usually did so anyway!

By this time the Schaeffers had become my friends, as well as my mentors. I learned a great deal, being with them and watching them. During one of Fran's visits to Boston he was to preach at Park Street Congregational Church. He had much earlier taken strong exception to the position of its pastor, Harold John Ockenga (1905–1985), criticizing his decision not to separate from his denomination. I rode in the car to the church with Fran. He was wrapped in a blanket, trying to get over a bad cold. He leaned over, clearly agitated, and told me, "Bill, I have fire in my bones." I was not sure what this was about. That night he preached an incredibly stirring message about holiness and fidelity. Most of the time he was shouting. It got louder and louder, and at the end, he said "and this stinks in the nostrils of God," then sat down, without the customary concluding prayer.

I would later learn that this was connected with a very deep-rooted anger over differences he held with Dr. Ockenga about ecclesiology. As we

---

[9] There were not many black people at Harvard at the time, although such luminaries as W. E. B. Du Bois had graduated from there. Later Harvard would boast one of the best "Afro-Am" departments in the country.

shall see, Fran held a strong separatist position and considered those who refused to separate over various issues to be compromisers. While he later would deeply regret some of the harshness with which he could treat those with whom he disagreed, he would never abandon his conviction about the purity of the visible church.

Another memorable encounter was a bit later, during a subsequent visit of Fran's to the States. I had decided to attend seminary after college, mostly to go deeper into the basics of my new-found faith. For various reasons, including the Schaeffers' encouragement, I chose to attend Westminster Theological Seminary, near Philadelphia. During my years as a student there in the late 1960s, President Edmund Clowney (1917–2005) determined to invite Schaeffer to our campus. Dr. Clowney had become quite taken with Schaeffer and the work of L'Abri. He was trying to move the seminary in a direction that would build more bridges with the outside world, and even, where feasible without compromise, reach out to evangelicals not necessarily from the strictly Reformed persuasion of the seminary. On this occasion he wanted to see if he could help mend some fences between two great men, Francis Schaeffer and Cornelius Van Til. Although Schaeffer had studied under Van Til at Westminster, he had come to express certain reservations about some of Van Til's emphases, which he deemed insufficiently cognizant of the need for evidences in arguments for the Christian faith. Van Til, on the other hand, worried that Schaeffer had slouched toward rationalism.

In 1968 President Clowney decided to put Schaeffer and Van Til in the same room and attempt a meeting of the minds. Although this ultimately was not really successful, at least the two of them were together and beginning to hash-out significant differences. They seemed to talk past each other. Apparently, at one point Van Til gave a bird's-eye view of the Reformed faith and presuppositional apologetics. After this speech Fran exclaimed that he wished he had recorded this and that he would have required every L'Abri worker to listen to it. There were certainly substantive disagreements between the two men, but as is often the case, innuendos and caricatures were as much in the mix as the questions themselves.[10]

---

[10] For an analysis of the similarities and contrasts between Van Til and Schaeffer, see my essay "Two Christian Warriors: Cornelius Van Til and Francis A. Schaeffer Compared," *Westminster Theological Journal* 57, no. 1 (Spring 1995): 57–80. Van Til was sharply critical of Schaeffer, though with obvious sympathies for him and his ministry. Van Til himself was plagued by criticisms of his views throughout his life. None were so serious or hurtful, perhaps, as those coming from Calvin Seminary, where, even after he was offered a position there, several potential colleagues strongly reproached him for his putative

Not only during the Schaeffers' trips to the States, but also in my frequent visits to L'Abri, I was able to learn a great deal. Such visits were made easy for me because our family lived in Geneva, right down the lake. For example, I continued to learn about prayer. Prayer was not only discussed but also practiced throughout the day, and in many varieties. L'Abri featured a number of special times of prayer. Once a year a day of prayer and fasting was held. A whole day! Then too, every week, we would all pause and go to a designated room for prayer. An extraordinary discipline, and a life-changing habit to nurture, prayer has become a precious way to deepen my primary relationship with God. I am still trying to do better at it, but it all began at L'Abri.

One initiative that many of us found very profitable was a day when we could take lunches and walk to a secluded place with a book. Though life was a bit less frenetic than it has become today, such a chance to get away, to be quiet, and to read more than a few pages at one sitting was precious.

Also at L'Abri, I learned that Sundays were very special. The church service and Schaeffer's sermons were astounding. His messages often lasted well over an hour, but we did not notice the time go by, and even wished they could last longer (a wish probably not shared by mothers with their young babies!). I was present for a number of memorable series. One was on the book of Job. After those powerful messages on Job I felt I knew the poor man personally. Such studies were far more compelling than many textbooks about the "problem of evil." I was also present when Schaeffer preached the series that would become the book *True Spirituality*, which will be central to the present volume.

Then, on a typical Sunday afternoon, after lunch (or "high tea") a group of us would go next door to Chalet Bellevue, at the time a home for victims of cerebral palsy. These beautiful people in wheelchairs, flailing their arms about, loved to sing the hymns led by Jane Stuart Smith, a retired opera singer who gave her life to the work of L'Abri. Treating everyone, disabled or not, as fully human, was one of the most remarkable testimonies from this place. Although it may sound insensitive to say this today, Schaeffer kept reminding us that we were all palsied, although some of us could hide our condition better than others.

lack of grace. See *Christian Apologetics Past and Present: A Primary Source Reader (Volume 2, from 1500)*, ed. William Edgar and K. Scott Oliphint (Wheaton: Crossway, 2011), 455.

**Further Involvements**

Barbara, my wife to be, went to L'Abri in the spring of 1966. She lived first in the Swiss L'Abri, then in the English branch for an entire year. She was a new believer, and this community was instrumental in solidifying her faith. Her first assignment was to help take care of Fran's mother, Bessie, whom the Schaeffers had moved to Switzerland after the death of her husband, Frank. Barbara vividly remembers playing checkers with her, often losing, as well as engaging in long, intense conversations. Her next assignment was to move to the British branch of L'Abri, which was begun in 1958 and was now directed by Ranald and Susan Macaulay. Barbara helped with their small children and generally assisted the family in various areas. She also was tasked with sending out the reel-to-reel tapes to those around the world who requested them.

Resources were always precarious. An incident stands out in Barbara's mind. One day Ranald announced that there was virtually no money. So for the next few days no one could have the helpings of food they desired. If you wanted a banana, you were asked to kindly eat only half of it. Coming from an affluent background, Barbara had thought nothing of eating a part of a banana and throwing the rest away. She learned a great deal from L'Abri as a faith mission, and such frugality had a lasting influence on her and the many who lived there. She was also deeply moved by the many dramatic answers to prayer she experienced in that place.

Fran wrote us the most meaningful letter when he received the news of our marriage, which the Schaeffers were unable to attend. He was a pastor through and through. He was quite sure our family would be the beautiful reflection of the love of Christ for his church (Eph. 5:22–33). As newlyweds, following the L'Abri style, we became very careful with our resources. We prayed for just about everything and tried to wait on the Lord for all our needs. After seminary, we became home missionaries for a Presbyterian church in Pennsylvania. This endeavor, too, was a faith mission, but thanks to L'Abri we had learned how to face the risks. Several months into this assignment we came to a crossroads. Although the L'Abri policy was not to ask anyone to come work there, it was clear Fran wanted us to come and help them out. After much prayer we decided against it. Our very dear friends Dick and Mardi Keyes, to whom I have dedicated this book, did go over, and have been involved in L'Abri ever since.

Instead of moving to Switzerland, our family felt called to Greenwich,

Connecticut, where we lived for nearly a decade, to teach at a day school. I taught French, philosophy, and music at the high school level and came to love that age very greatly. We were able to lead a Christian fellowship and to connect to an independent school ministry called FOCUS. David Bragdon, Jonathan's brother, was the math teacher there. The head of the school was kind enough to encourage me all along the way. He appointed me chair of the music department and sent me to the Dalcroze School in Geneva in the summer of 1974 for further training in music education. So we lived with my parents, and of course had several chances to visit the Schaeffers during those months.

As it happened, Fran was busily preparing an address he was to give at the very first Lausanne International Congress on World Evangelization (July 16–25). He spoke on "Form and Freedom in the Church." The paper stressed the need for sound doctrine, the need to "answer honest questions with honest answers," but also the need for true spirituality, and for "the beauty of human relationships."[11] His thinking on true spirituality was by now fully crystallized. One aspect of the paper was the remark that the Protestant Reformation, marvelous as it was, had overlooked two major problems: race and money (or "affluency," as he termed it). He read his paper to a riveted audience. This entire congress was dedicated to getting the balance right between evangelism and doing justice. It would produce the Lausanne Covenant, which notably sought to redress an imbalance in the evangelical approach to the social dimension of the gospel. Schaeffer was a key part of it. Justice was never incidental to him, but an integral part of the gospel.

Also memorable for me was my involvement in the film *How Should We Then Live?* The title is a quote from Ezekiel 33:10. The film (1977) came with a companion volume (1976). The two are parallel, though not at all points. The overall concern of the series is to examine the flow of Western history in order to determine where we are today and then to suggest changes that need to be made so that the world could be a better place for the next generations. A sweeping journey from the Greeks and Romans through the present, it is a summary statement of much of what Francis Schaeffer had taught over the years. It has a distinctly Cold War feeling, with warnings against tyrannical government and descriptions of the menace of communism in the later portions. It also has hints of the

---

[11] See http://www.lausanne.org/documents/lau1docs/0368.pdf.

view that understands the Founding Fathers of America to have held to a "Christian consensus," a view that has several forms, centering on the degree to which the Founding Fathers were self-consciously Christian. Fran had previously engaged in a vigorous debate with historian Mark Noll over the proper interpretation of this period. George Marsden, a specialist in American colonial history, also weighed in.[12]

Though at first reluctant, Fran was eventually convinced to make this film by his son, Franky, together with Billy Zeoli of Gospel Films, Inc. Billy is the son of Anthony Zeoli, into whose tent ministry Fran wandered as a young man, an experience that would help define his fledgling Christian faith, as we shall see. Franky and Billy appealed to Fran's desire to get the message out to a larger audience. They persuaded him that the film could be a corrective to certain series sponsored by public television. Fran had become concerned that many of the most influential PBS and BBC series, such as Kenneth Clark's *Civilisation*, were prejudiced against the historic Christian position.

My own involvement was with the music featured in the series. I am not sure of the internal politics that led to their employing me, since the name Jane Stuart Smith appears on the list of credits, not mine. In retrospect, I am just as glad. All in all, it was a learning experience. The final version of the film was reduced from thirteen to eleven episodes because of various problems.

To be honest, it is not the best documentary ever produced. Various portions of it lack professionalism. In one episode Thomas Aquinas, a bald monk, is copying a text from Aristotle, and Fran bursts into the room with some weighty words about Thomas's dependence on the Greek philosopher and his nature/grace scheme. Perhaps for good reason, the series never made it to public television. At the same time, nothing quite like it had ever been done by an evangelical Christian. It was shown all over America and beyond, thanks to willing friends and supporters. A number of us hosted these events, and they became excellent discussion points.

## L'Abri Today

Today, L'Abri lives on. There are ten residential L'Abris around the world, as well as a number of nonresidential ones. Barbara and I have been involved,

---

[12] An account of this debate can be found in Barry Hankins, *Francis Schaeffer and the Shaping of Evangelical America* (Grand Rapids: Eerdmans, 2008), 211–27.

off and on, in several of them. Each of them has a different character, owing to its particular history and leadership. In the nonresidential L'Abris, events and discussions are held, but no overnight facilities are provided.

The official website describes L'Abri as having four emphases and a final goal.[13] (1) Christianity is objectively true and the Bible is God's written word to mankind; which means that biblical Christianity can be rationally defended and honest questions are welcome. (2) Because Christianity is true, it speaks to all of life and not to some narrowly religious sphere; therefore, much of the material produced by L'Abri is aimed at helping develop a Christian perspective on the arts, politics, and the social sciences, and so forth. (3) In our relationship with God, true spirituality is seen in lives that by grace are free to be fully human rather than in trying to live "on some higher spiritual plane" or in "some grey negative way." (4) L'Abri takes the reality of the fall seriously, and declares that until Christ returns, we and our world are disfigured by sin. Finally, the statement adds, while L'Abri takes the mind seriously, it is not a place for intellectuals only. L'Abri is as much concerned for living as for thinking. Within these overall emphases, each of these branches has a distinctive character, often shaped by the leadership.

A number of L'Abri centers were run by the Schaeffer children or by associates close to the heart of the work. Indeed, each of the Schaeffer children has taken their parents' life and heritage in a particular direction. Prisca and her husband, John, stayed in Huémoz and continue to help with the ongoing work. John has had some apparent doctrinal differences with official L'Abri teaching, yet he stays on and is tremendously helpful. Susan and Ranald Macaulay are living in Cambridge, England, and after years of working at L'Abri, now pour their lives into a work called Christian Heritage, which consists of courses, tours, seminars, and debates around the subject of the truth of the gospel. Ranald loves to take visitors around the university and show them mementos of the Christian past of that great center for learning: John Newton's rooms, Faraday's laboratory, the White Horse Inn, and so on. Debbie and Udo Middelmann left L'Abri to establish a work called the Francis Schaeffer Foundation, in Gryon, across the valley from Huémoz.

The Schaeffer's son, Franky (now called Frank), married to Genie, is the most controversial of the Schaeffer children. He is a filmmaker, an author, a painter, and a social critic. He left the Protestant communion and

---

[13] http://www.labri.org/.

has embraced Eastern Orthodoxy in its Antiochian expression. Also, he
has developed rather a cottage industry of books that combine sensitive,
personal insights into life with his parents with rather caustic critiques of
many people, including his mother and father. In an odd historiography,
Frank today accepts the blame for guiding his dad into collaboration with
the evangelical right, which he now largely repudiates. While many of us
believe there are serious problems with his reading of L'Abri and his parents' work, it is hard not to sympathize with a young man brought up in
such a pressure cooker. He says, in *Crazy for God*: "I was in the work, but
not of it. The intrusion of the students, the hurly-burly of the comings and
goings, the growing crowds of people who came on Sunday to church in
the summer, the constant noise around the house, everything made me
hate where I lived—and love it."[14]

Nonfamily members too have excelled in their development of
L'Abri into the next generations. Dick and Mardi Keyes, at the L'Abri in
Southborough, Massachusetts, just outside Boston, have developed
extraordinary material on numerous subjects related to Christian apologetics, from studies on identity, to issues such as heroism, cynicism, and
gender. Larry and Nancy Snyder, working in the Rochester, Minnesota,
branch, have contributed greatly, including their sponsorship of an annual
L'Abri conference in February, which attracts hundreds of people. The original L'Abri, in Huémoz, has seven chalets, each with a staff member, welcoming scores of visitors each year. In addition, branches exist in Holland,
England, Sweden, Korea, Canada, Germany, and Brazil.[15]

Francis Schaeffer's legacy is still being felt. His impact is still being
evaluated as well, and probably will be for years to come. In my teaching
and writing I find myself constantly referring back to what I learned from
L'Abri and the work of Fran and Edith Schaeffer, as well as that of Hans
Rookmaaker (1922–1977), Fran's close collaborator, and the founder of the
Dutch L'Abri. Each of us who came of age spiritually within the L'Abri ethos
have moved on and developed our own specific emphases. But the ties are
deep and the culture of L'Abri, as well as the ideas generated, have stayed
with us, and defined us.

---

[14] Frank Schaeffer, *Crazy for God: How I Grew Up as One of the Elect, Helped Found the Religious Right, and Lived to Take All (or Almost All) of It Back* (New York: Carroll & Graf, 2007), 218. See also Frank Schaeffer, *Portofino: A Novel* (New York: Da Capo, 1974); *Saving Grandma: A Novel* (New York: Da Capo, 2004); *Zermatt: A Novel* (New York: Da Capo, 2004); *Sex, Mom, and God: How the Bible's Strange Take on Sex Led to Crazy Politics—and How I Learned to Love Women (and Jesus) Anyway* (New York: Da Capo, 2011).
[15] http://www.labri.org/today.html.

PART I

# THE MAN AND HIS TIMES

CHAPTER 2

# THE JOURNEY TO L'ABRI

*Schaeffer found that only the Bible did justice to the way the universe is, and to questions arising out of its realities.*

UDO MIDDELMANN

## The Early Years

Francis Schaeffer's unique personality as well as his views were the fruit of a unique journey. The story of the Schaeffers and of L'Abri has often been told.[1] The present volume is not a biography but a study of Francis Schaeffer's approach to spirituality, although of course the two are intertwined. Here follows, then, the briefest account of his life.

His grandfather, Franz Schaeffer, emigrated to America in 1869, after fighting in the Franco-Prussian wars. Desiring to turn over a new leaf, he burned most of the family papers, making the work of the biographers more difficult. He died in an accident working on the railroad in

---

[1] Readers are referred to several sources regarding the life of Francis Schaeffer and his family. There are a couple of autobiographies by Edith Schaeffer. These are well worth reading. *L'Abri* (London: Norfolk Press, 1969) was the first. Her more extended work, *The Tapestry: The Life and Times of Francis and Edith Schaeffer* (Waco, TX: Word, 1981), is a combination of a detailed reporting on the Schaeffer family, intertwined with reflections on various issues, including theological and biblical ones, as well as the questions of the day. It is also worth looking through the correspondence. Many of the letters remain in archives kept at the Francis A. Schaeffer Foundation, which is in the trust of Southeastern Baptist Theological Seminary in Wake Forest, North Carolina. Other papers and memorabilia are kept at Covenant Theological Seminary's Francis Schaeffer Institute in St. Louis, and at Wheaton College in Wheaton, Illinois. For a good sampling of the correspondence, see Lane T. Dennis, ed., *The Letters of Francis Schaeffer: Spiritual Reality in the Personal Christian Life* (Wheaton, IL: Crossway, 1986). Edith Schaeffer's family letters also give a unique window on the life at L'Abri. A number have been published as *With Love, Edith: The L'Abri Family Letters, 1948–1960* (San Francisco: Harper & Row, 1988); and *Dear Family: The L'Abri Family Letters 1961–1986* (San Francisco: Harper & Row, 1989). Frank Schaeffer's accounts of his upbringing and his

Philadelphia, leaving a three-year-old little boy, known as Frank (Francis Schaeffer's father).

Frank developed a strong work ethic and joined the Navy while still in his teens, learning to ride the rigging in any kind of weather. Frank was a Lutheran when he married Bessie, who worshiped at the local Evangelical Free Church. It is not certain how seriously or personally they took the Christian faith. Later, they clearly became followers of Christ. Together they worked hard to pull themselves up from the kind of poverty their parents had known. They determined to have only one child. He turned out to be Francis August Schaeffer IV, born on January 30, 1912.

The lad grew up in stark circumstances. His father never went beyond third grade, and there were no books at home. That did not mean his dad was not a thinking person. On the contrary, as Fran would often remind us, working-class people are often very deep intellectually, even though they may not be able to name the major philosophers. Accordingly, Fran was far more critical of the "bourgeois" middle class than either the intellectual elite or the working class. Nor was there much entertainment for the family, except the occasional trip to Atlantic City. If Fran had friends, they only rarely visited or played with him. Much later he would be diagnosed with dyslexia. This could have amusing results. He called Mahalia Jackson "Matilda" Jackson. The galaxy was the "galacacy." Affluence was "affluency." Spontaneity became "spontanuity," and so on. For young Fran, however, there was probably nothing amusing about it, since schools were far from understanding about learning disabilities in those days. Despite that, a number of kindly teachers took an interest in the young man and worked patiently with him. Fran especially remembered a Mrs. Lidie C. Bell at Roosevelt Junior High School, who taught the children something

---

exposés on inside secrets are of mixed value. But the interested reader may particularly want to look at his *Crazy for God: How I Grew Up as One of the Elect, Helped Found the Religious Right, and Lived to Take All (or Almost All) of It Back* (New York: Carroll & Graf, 2007), mentioned earlier. Then there are a number of biographies by nonfamily members. My favorite is by Colin Duriez, *Francis Schaeffer: An Authentic Life* (Wheaton, IL: Crossway, 2008). There is also Barry Hankins's provocative *Francis Schaeffer and the Shaping of Evangelical America* (Grand Rapids: Eerdmans, 2008), also mentioned above. An earlier, somewhat hagiographical account is L. G. Parkhurst, *Francis A. Schaeffer: The Man and His Message* (Eastbourne: Kingsway, 1986). Finally, there are places in other biographies, histories, and encyclopedia entries where we have a window on the Schaeffers' life from various authors. Some of these were close friends. My favorite is a two-part course given by Jerram Barrs of Covenant Theological Seminary, "Francis A. Schaeffer: The Early Years," and "Francis A. Schaeffer: The Later Years," available at http://www.covenantseminary.edu/resources/#!/courses-francis-schaeffer-the-early-years and . . . the -later-years. Another example is by Dr. C. Everett Koop, who coauthored a book and a film with Francis Schaeffer. Koop has an autobiography in which his colleague has a part, *Koop: The Memoirs of America's Family Doctor* (New York: Random House, 1991). Michael Hamilton's article, "The Dissatisfaction of Francis Schaeffer," *Christianity Today*, March 3, 1997, 22–30, is insightful.

about the history of art, a subject that would become central to Fran's thinking throughout his life.

As was expected, at least for social reasons, Fran went to church. He chose the First Presbyterian Church of Germantown, largely because it was the meeting place for his Boy Scout troop. But the preaching was mostly liberal and lacked satisfactory answers about the issues of life. Fran was intellectually curious. He had somehow picked up a book about Greek philosophy and was deeply taken by it. He was fairly certain there was not much to the Christian faith. But he decided in fairness to read through the Bible so that should he reject it, he could do so with integrity.

The opposite effect was produced. Quite on his own, he decided that the Bible answered many of the basic questions raised by Greek philosophy. By September 1930, he was able to say in his diary, "All truth is from the Bible." Edith Schaeffer, in her extensive biography *The Tapestry*, compared Fran's conversion to the story of a shepherd boy by Kristína Royová.[2] In her *Sunshine Country* a young man discovers the Gospel of Mark in a cave in the hills and thinks no one else knows about this amazing text. Fran thought he had come upon something quite unknown. He told Edith, later in life, "What rang the bell for me was the answers in Genesis, and that with these you had answers—real answers—and without these there were no answers either in philosophies or in the religion I had heard preached."[3]

This rather private experience was soon to have a more public expression. Fran happened on an old-fashioned gospel meeting where evangelist Anthony Zeoli (father of Billy Zeoli, the collaborator on the film *How Should We Then Live?*) preached in a compelling way. The content was along the same lines that Fran had thought had been his own personal discovery about the Bible. He wrote in his diary, ". . . have decided to give my whole life to Christ unconditionally."[4] From the start he felt called to the ministry. This pursuit was not appreciated by his parents, who were rather suspicious of professional clerics. Yet his father recognized Fran's determination and eventually gave in, even supporting him. After Fran worked in a number of manual jobs, as well as studying engineering at Drexel College at night, the urge to enter the ministry became so strong that he determined, upon the advice of a trusted elder, to attend Hampden-Sydney College, a first-rate Presbyterian school in Virginia, pursuing preministerial studies.

---

[2] In *The Tapestry*, Edith mistakenly attributes the story to Christina Rossetti.
[3] Edith Schaeffer, *The Tapestry*, 52.
[4] Ibid., 55.

His father, contrary to his instincts, was again impressed with Fran's determination, and so paid the first semester's tuition.

At first, college was not easy for Fran. The practice of hazing was
accepted, and his classmates were particularly hard on preministerial
students. Fran's working-class background earned him the nickname
"Philly," and he had to learn to defend himself against his rather more aris-
tocratic tormentors. Though only 5'6" he was strong and athletic. The hazing ended one day when Fran overcame his persecutor in a serious fight.
He could also use his strength for evangelistic purposes. For example, he
regularly rescued drunk students on Saturday nights (there was plenty
of alcohol around, despite Prohibition in America) and helped them back
to their rooms on condition they would attend church with him the next
morning. He excelled in his studies, particularly philosophy and Greek.
He would graduate magna cum laude.

On his first summer vacation, Fran met his wife-to-be, Edith Seville.
She had grown up in China, her parents serving with the China Inland
Mission, founded by Hudson Taylor. The Sevilles had recently moved to
Germantown, in the northwest section of Philadelphia, where Edith's father
George began editing the mission's magazine, *China's Millions*. Already a
character, Edith had determined that if she were to become a missionary,
she would never look like one! She loved clothes. She loved music and dance,
and was not to be typecast. As circumstances would have it, Fran and Edith
both attended the same meeting at the First Presbyterian Church to hear a
Unitarian speaker attempt to dismiss the claims that Christ was God in the
flesh and that the Bible was God's word. During the question period Fran
rose up to explain how Christ had changed his life. Edith then also rose to
speak, citing J. Gresham Machen and Robert Dick Wilson, two remarkable
evangelical scholars teaching at Westminster Theological Seminary, down
the street. That night, after ordering her to break a date, Fran walked her
home. Over the summer their friendship developed into love. They wrote
every day. They were intellectually well matched and deeply in love. They
married July 6, 1935. Fran was twenty-three and Edith twenty years old.
She left college before graduating in order better to support Fran.

### Seminary

Following his conviction that he should become a minister, Fran decided
to attend seminary. At Edith's behest, he applied to Westminster and was

accepted for the fall of 1935. These were the heady days of the fundamentalist-modernist controversies. Though reluctant to call himself a fundamentalist, the most scholarly defender of historic Christian faith was J. Gresham Machen (1881–1937). Machen had taught New Testament at Princeton Theological Seminary from 1915 to 1929, interrupted briefly by his work in France with the YMCA during World War I, a war he strongly opposed. His best-known books are *The Origin of Paul's Religion* (1921), *Christianity and Liberalism* (1923), and *What Is Faith?* (1925). Each of these argued for the historic Christian position over against liberal Christianity. Edith had been greatly influenced by these writings. Princeton Seminary had been a bastion of orthodoxy since its founding in 1812. Such remarkable scholars as Archibald Alexander, Charles Hodge, Benjamin B. Warfield, and Geerhardus Vos taught there over the years.

Princeton Seminary was ultimately controlled by the General Assembly of the Presbyterian Church (U.S.A.). But a growing division occurred in the 1920s, culminating in the Assembly's appointing two trustees who had signed the Auburn Affirmation, a more liberal statement of faith. Several faculty promptly left Princeton and founded Westminster Theological Seminary in Philadelphia. These men were to have a considerable influence on the young Francis Schaeffer. They included Robert Dick Wilson (Semitic philology and Old Testament), J. G. Machen (New Testament), Oswald Allis (Old Testament history and exegesis), R. B. Kuiper (systematic theology), Ned Stonehouse (New Testament), Allan MacRae (Semitic philology and, later, biblical archeology), Cornelius Van Til (apologetics), and Paul Woolley (registrar and professor of church history).

Though in theological continuity with the "Old Princeton," Westminster launched into a number of initiatives that would make it more than a carbon copy of the older institution. For one, it was to be independent from any denomination. Being free from denominational control, Westminster hoped to avoid the problems that had occurred at Princeton. Also, this arrangement would allow faculty from several denominations to teach, as long as they could subscribe to the documents known as the Westminster Standards, the historic confession and catechisms of the Presbyterian church.

For another, the new seminary also determined not to take sides on two issues, a decision that would lead to controversy in its early years: the millennial question and the so-called Christian liberties. The millennial question involved the interpretation of Revelation 20:2–3, which states that Satan would be bound for a thousand years. According to the "premillennial" position, Christ will come first to establish a rule over the earth literally for a thousand years. The "amillennial" view states that this is a symbolic number signifying the present limiting of Satan's powers. Then, the "postmillennial" view holds that through the preaching of the gospel, a thousand-year reign of Christ will be established prior to the end of the world. At the time of the founding there were professors at Westminster who represented each of these three views. The issue of Christian liberty meant forbidding alcohol, smoking, the theater, dancing, and games of chance. The idea was that though Christians might be free to indulge in them, for the sake of being a good witness to a degenerating world it was urgent to abstain. While few Westminster professors actually indulged in these practices (the exception being John Murray, who upon occasion is said to have enjoyed a glass of single malt whiskey) the seminary believed the Bible encourages moderation, not abstinence.

From the beginning, Westminster's scholars were more than defensive. They made significant innovations in their disciplines. Stonehouse would become an outstanding expert on the order of the Synoptic Gospels. Van Til forged the way toward "presuppositional" apologetics and also mounted a strong critique of Karl Barth (1886–1968) and neoorthodoxy. In a few years the approach to the Bible known as "biblical theology" would reign in the Bible departments. This meant looking at developments in the history of redemption as progressive, culminating in the advent of Jesus Christ, in the manner of Princeton notable Geerhardus Vos, as opposed to reading the Bible flatly, as a dictionary. Years later, Westminster also would be on the cutting edge of biblical counseling and urban missions.

The years Fran attended Westminster were full of turmoil. Machen had founded the Independent Board for Presbyterian Foreign Missions (IBPFM) in 1933, which was decidedly more orthodox than the official Presbyterian mission board. For refusing to endorse the official board, though, Machen was defrocked from the ministry. After his appeal failed, he led a number of people into the formation of a new denomination, the Presbyterian Church of America, soon to be renamed the Orthodox Presbyterian Church (OPC). Fran immediately withdrew his own credentials in the larger Presbyterian Church and joined the smaller group. He was grieved that some others, such as Harold Ockenga, as already mentioned, did not. Dr. Ockenga was the cofounder of Fuller Theological Seminary, which attempted to be more inclusive and more in touch with current studies, as it was thought, than the separatist seminaries. On January 1, 1937, on a trip to North Dakota, Machen died suddenly of pneumonia, basically from exhaustion. He was buried in Baltimore. The seminary's driving force was gone. This was quite devastating for many, including the Schaeffers. As a matter of historical interest, Machen gave his very last exam to Fran, who had to sit for it by Machen's sick bed.

Soon thereafter, the Schaeffers came to a critical decision. Fran and Edith had become increasingly concerned about what they saw to be a lack of holiness in the seminary family. They accused relationships there of being "harsh and ugly." Fran would later dub such an approach as "cold orthodoxy." They believed that Westminster had become virtually "hyper-Calvinist," going beyond what Scripture clearly taught and confusing divine election with determinism. Also, as mentioned, though Westminster was officially neutral on details of eschatology (the last things), the Schaeffers were decidedly premillennialists. Beyond simply their particular views of what would happen in the end times, premillennialists believed that the larger question of the authority of the Bible was at stake. If you did not accept the millennium as a literal number of years, then what will you be reducing to symbolism next? Genesis 1–11? The resurrection?

An important nuance must be made here. Francis Schaeffer believed in *historic* premillennialism, not *dispensationalist* premillennialism. Without going into detail, classic dispensationalism holds that redemptive history should be parsed into seven episodes, or dispensations, in each of which believers relate to God and his salvation somewhat differently. A majority of dispensationalists believe in the "rapture" of Christians just before a great period of tribulation, after which comes the millennial reign. *Historic* premillennialism takes its name from the fact that several of the church fathers taught that there would be a visible kingdom of God established on the earth for a thousand years, just after the return of Christ and before the future final judgment. However, historic premillennialists do not accept the details spelled out in the dispensationalist version of premillennialism. George Eldon Ladd, Walter Martin, J. Barton Payne, and a number of impressive evangelicals, for example, held to historic premillennialism.[5]

---

[5] These concerns with "prophecy" were enormously discussed in those days. While it is certain that Fran's views were along the lines of historic premillennialism, many of us can remember Edith speculating on such things as the "secret rapture," wherein believers would be suddenly swept out of the

Besides their eschatological commitments, the Schaeffers and their group had come to believe that truly committed Christians should separate denominationally from mixed ones, which they called accommodationist. Machen and the founders of the OPC were certainly separatists, but a more radical minority was emerging, which began to identify itself as "The Movement." This smaller group also opposed the Christian liberties and thus would refrain, as mentioned above, from conduct that would "spoil their testimony." The prohibition against dancing was particularly difficult for Edith, who loved to dance. Though most who held this view recognized that the Bible does not proscribe such liberties, they felt in light of the moral problems in the surrounding culture that it was best to avoid them. Fran would later be known to enjoy a glass of wine, and certainly to attend the cinema. And in the right setting, Edith used to demonstrate her dancing skills for us!

Matters came to a head in the General Assembly of the new church, held in early June 1937. Tempers flared and suspicions were voiced about who was really orthodox. In the end, this minority left the OPC and founded the Bible Presbyterian Church. They also began a new seminary. Faith Theological Seminary, in Wilmington, Delaware, would continue to teach Reformed theology, along with premillennialism and abstinence from Christian liberties. In 1938 the new denomination modified chapter 33 of the Westminster Confession of Faith to lend support to premillennialism. Among the seminary's leaders were Allan MacRae, who was designated president, and J. Oliver Buswell Jr., then the president of Wheaton College, who for a time took on both jobs. Also in the group was the fiery Carl McIntire, with whom Fran would eventually tangle.

As an aside, it should be pointed out that many in this new church and seminary were less committed to Van Til's presuppositionalist apologetics and more open to some combination of views, including "evidentialism," the approach that takes biblical data and other empirical evidences for the Christian faith at face value, without the need to ground them in presuppositions.[6] Such evidences can be within the Bible or from realms such as

world, resulting in such catastrophes as pilots disappearing and airplanes tumbling to earth. For further reference, see, *The Encyclopedia of Millennialism and Millennial Movements*, ed. Richard Landes (Boston: Routledge, 2000).

[6] The interested reader can delve deeper into these different schools by consulting the considerable literature on the subject. See Bradley J. Longfield, *The Presbyterian Controversy: Fundamentalists, Modernists, and Moderates* (New York: Oxford University Press, 1991); D. G. Hart, *The Old-Time Religion in*

archeology. But the point is that they are self-evident, or neutral, rather than encompassed by a God-centered framework within which they make sense. Though himself always claiming to be a presuppositionalist, albeit somewhat eclectic in practice, Fran went with the new seminary and the new denomination. Fran graduated in the class of 1938 and was the first minister to be ordained in the Bible Presbyterian Church.

### Churches and a Growing Family

The Schaeffers spent the next ten years in pastoral ministry. With their young daughter, Janet Priscilla, born June 18, 1938, they first took a church in Grove City, in western Pennsylvania. The area was mostly industrial. There was also an excellent Christian liberal arts college. The congregation was small, but after a few years of hard work, the Schaeffers saw numbers grow. Many people came to faith. The Schaeffers had a particular gift for reaching children. They started a local chapter of the Miracle Book Club out of their home. Edith would later understand this work to be the very beginning of the L'Abri-like ministry that would develop throughout their career. Susan, their second daughter, was born May 28, 1941. Fran tried to be a good father. Yet he was also deeply involved not only in the local church but also the denomination. Even with his extraordinary energy it was hard to juggle family, church, and denomination.

After a successful three years in Grove City the Schaeffers moved east to Chester, Pennsylvania, where Fran became the associate minister at a large Bible Presbyterian church. He was very fond of Abraham Lathem, the senior pastor. Fran contributed greatly to the church, being able, among other things, to reach out to the working-class folks in the congregation. In 1941 America got involved in the World War that was ravaging Europe and then the Pacific. This would mean blackouts and ration stamps. Life was hard for most Americans. Pastors were considered special, since they were shepherds of the people who stayed home; for example, they were allowed to drive at night with the car lights on. An especially joyous event occurred that same year: Fran's father, Frank, became a believer.

Also in 1941 the American Council of Christian Churches (ACCC) was founded. The group was a conservative answer to the Federal Council of Churches (now the National Council of Churches), which was affili-

*Modern America: Evangelical Protestantism in the Twentieth Century* (Lanham, MD: Ivan R. Dee, 2003); and George M. Marsden, *Understanding Fundamentalism and Evangelicalism* (Grand Rapids: Eerdmans, 1991).

ated with the World Council of Churches, deemed to be doctrinally lax, even heretical and dangerous. Member churches in the ACCC had to have refused participation in the broader National and World Councils of Churches. The ACCC would become an important venue for Schaeffer's activities. Thanks to its mission Fran would be able to travel to Europe, where his eyes opened to the scene there in the aftermath of the war.

In 1942 Fran wrote a white paper for the Bible Presbyterian Church entitled *Our System of Doctrine*, outlining the distinctives of the Bible Presbyterian denomination.[7] The paper described it as "a doctrinal church," one that was Protestant, supernaturalist, evangelical, and particularist—meaning that they confessed the absolute sovereignty of God for salvation and separated from those who did not. He called this separatist stand "doctrine in action." In addition, the Bible Presbyterians were premillennialists. While Schaeffer was careful to recognize the Synod's official "eschatological liberty," it is clear that the general consensus of the church was premillennialism, a doctrine, he said, "we believe . . . with all of our heart." This little tract gives a fair idea of where Francis Schaeffer stood in those days. Ten years later he would rethink this style of separatism—not separation itself but the coldness with which he and many colleagues approached people with whom they disagreed.

After only two years in Chester, the family moved to St. Louis, Missouri. The year was 1943, and America was plunged in the Second World War. The Schaeffers stayed in St. Louis five years, Fran's longest pastoral charge. He was thirty-one and Edith twenty-eight. Their third daughter, Deborah, was born May 3, 1945. First Bible Presbyterian Church was in an urban setting and enjoyed considerable diversity, which pleased the Schaeffers. The war was coming to an end, but Fran was deeply concerned over the momentous events going on in Europe. One can imagine many reasons for his interest in the Old World. It could be that his German ancestry made him especially aware of particulars of the war. Similarly, he may have been concerned about the higher criticism of the Bible, much of which was German. Furthermore, Fran was greatly troubled about the fate of the Jewish people, whom he loved deeply. He often preached and wrote against anti-Semitism. And he cherished the arts, which had flourished in Europe.

So, while he worked hard as a pastor in St. Louis, his heart was being

---

[7] Adopted from a paper read at the General Synod of the Bible Presbyterian Church, St. Louis, Missouri, 1942; published by the Publications Committee of the Bible Presbyterian Church, Philadelphia.

drawn to Europe. During their ministry at First Bible Presbyterian the Schaeffers continued to work extensively with children. With rallies and summer Bible schools, as well as the creation of a Christian version of Boy Scouts and Girl Scouts, the Schaeffers went about reaching out to children and their parents with great energy and imagination. One of their endeavors, Children for Christ, established in 1945, could well have become a full-time enterprise.

## To Switzerland

The events in the next few years will have to be collapsed into a few short paragraphs, though they deserve a fuller accounting. In the summer of 1947 the Independent Board for Presbyterian Foreign Missions, now controlled by McIntire and the separatists, agreed to send Fran on an exploratory journey to Europe in order to determine what the needs of the local churches might be. At issue were the inroads made by the increasing presence of theological liberalism, as well as neoorthodoxy. The mission was especially concerned for the children of churches that were unaware of these theological trends. Edith and the girls moved to Cape Cod for the summer, and their friend Elmer Smick took over Fran's pastoral responsibilities.

The trip was long and exhausting. In the three summer months Fran traveled all over Europe, clocking hundreds of interviews.[8] During this time he was able either to meet or hear a number of influential theologians of varying stripes, including André Lamorte, Willem Visser't Hooft, Reinhold Niebuhr, Ole Hallesby, G. C. Berkouwer, and Martyn Lloyd-Jones. Interestingly, Lloyd-Jones would himself stand for separation when he famously called for evangelicals to leave denominations belonging to the World Council of Churches in 1966 (which meant a well-publicized contention with John R. W. Stott, the leading British evangelical Anglican). But when he met with Francis Schaeffer, he expressed strong reservations about the lack of kindness he saw in his movement, a diagnosis that Fran would eventually share. When he was not in meetings Fran visited the great museums and studied the architecture of the European cities, making a dream come true. It was upon the return journey that the DC-4 would feather its props and then be miraculously

---

[8] A blow-by-blow account is given in Duriez, *Francis Schaeffer*, 64–70.

delivered, becoming the vivid illustration of prayer answered that I heard on my first evening at L'Abri.

Fran returned thoroughly fatigued. After being nursed back to full strength by the ever-patient and loving Edith, he went around various American churches giving talks based on what he had learned abroad. Out of these presentations developed a critique of the intellectual climate in Europe in relation to modern theology. Eventually these ideas crystallized into some standard lectures, then the books.

Though Fran greatly enjoyed being a local pastor, he received numerous invitations from the churches he had visited abroad, and heard what amounted to a "Macedonian call" to come over and help them. Thus, in response, he and Edith made the momentous decision to become missionaries to Europe, serving with the Independent Board. The long-term plan was to live in Switzerland and from there carry out ministries such as Fran had tested out during his summer abroad. Their duties fell under the call to represent the Independent Board in whatever way the Lord was leading them.

So Fran preached his last sermon in St. Louis, and in February 1948 the Schaeffers collected all their belongings and made their way to Philadelphia, where they would live with Bessie Schaeffer for six months before leaving for Europe. Living with his mother proved a difficult experience. (Over two decades later, she would be moved to Switzerland and live with the Schaeffers, and my wife, Barbara, would be assigned to help take care of her.)

One incident occurring during this time in Philadelphia, though unpleasant, augured well for the future. Priscilla contracted a strange illness, causing her to vomit violently. At the Philadelphia Children's Hospital the doctors were baffled. A thirty-two-year-old physician named C. Everett Koop walked into the room, examined Priscilla, and diagnosed her with "mesenteric adenitis," a disease he had just been studying. He had learned that most often the condition could be cured by the removal of the appendix, for reasons not clear to medical science. Edith mentioned to Dr. Koop that they were moving to Switzerland to become missionaries. Koop had just become a believer through the ministry of Tenth Presbyterian Church on Seventeenth and Spruce Streets. He performed the operation himself. Just before he wheeled Priscilla into the operating room, a telegram came in from Fran, who was traveling in Nashville, saying, "Dear

Priscilla, Remember underneath are the everlasting arms. Love, Daddy."[9] Dr. Koop was deeply moved by the marvel of this kind of faith. Later, Fran and he would meet and forge a friendship that led, among other things, to casting the film *Whatever Happened to the Human Race?*

The family set sail for Europe early in August 1948. Their very first assignment was to help organize meetings in Amsterdam, in preparation for a new group, the International Council of Christian Churches (ICCC), inspired in large part by Carl McIntire (1906–2002). This was to be the international extension of the ACCC. It also was meant to be a sort of conservative alternative to the World Council of Churches, mentioned earlier, which happened to be inaugurated just after the ICCC, also in Amsterdam. (It appeared to some that McIntire was deliberately shadowing the larger group in order to needle it.) During these meetings Fran met Hans Rookmaaker, a graduate student in art history at the Free University of Amsterdam who was working on his dissertation about Gauguin and synthetist art theories. Rookmaaker would eventually become a professor at the same university. He soon became Fran's closest friend. Amusingly, the two of them met in the ICCC office, where Hans's fiancée, Anky Huitker, was helping out as secretary. Hans was to take her home after work. He spotted Fran and thought that he could talk to the American about jazz music, on which he was already a considerable expert. They talked on and on, covering not only jazz but many other subjects, eventually roaming around the streets of Amsterdam till late at night. They came back at 4:00 in the morning, quite forgetting about escorting Anky home!

I have reflected on this friendship over the years. Earlier on I was fairly convinced that Schaeffer's knowledge of art and music owed enormous amounts to Rookmaaker, almost as a one-way street. I have since come to believe that while Schaeffer was less the scholar than his friend, he nevertheless had amassed a considerable understanding of the arts on his own. Furthermore, God used Fran and Edith in the Rookmaakers' life at a time when they were going through a period of spiritual dryness, caused in part by the culture of their own "separated" churches in Holland. The two would continue to inspire one another over the years. Fran once told me that he and Hans were so close, he was never sure which one had generated some of their best ideas first! As close friends do, they fussed from time to time. Hans once expressed frustration to me that Fran had not acknowledged

---

[9] Edith Schaeffer, *The Tapestry*, 282.

him in a couple of publications. But he planned to respond by not acknowl-edging Fran in some paper he had written. Puerile? Never mind, they were as close as could possibly be. At the memorial service after Rookmaaker's untimely death in 1977 Fran recounted their times together, and "tears flowed unashamedly."[10]

After the events in Amsterdam, the family moved to Lausanne, in the canton de Vaud. The Schaeffers spoke throughout Europe in an effort to begin Children for Christ chapters in various places. They tirelessly tried to warn the churches of the dangers of liberalism and neoorthodoxy. A new-found love for skiing took them to the mountain village of Champéry. This was a most welcome change for the children. The family ended up renting a chalet there over the summer in 1949. Soon, they loved Champéry so much, it seemed agreeable to move there permanently. For the next few years, beginning in November, Chalet des Frênes in this lovely mountain village was their home and their base of operations.

During these years Fran continued to visit much of Europe. The Schaeffers also launched a number of activities for young people in the chalet. Regular visitors included young women from the nearby finish-ing school, as well as locals and assorted acquaintances.[11] This ministry at home took on a life of its own. There were usually tea and cookies, a warm fire, and then intense discussions about the Christian world-and-life view with any guest that showed up. Local church meetings began to become somewhat regular. Fran was invited to preach in Champéry on Christmas eve, a tradition that would continue long after they moved to the other side of the valley. One year, when I was skiing there with my parents, I took them to that service in the hopes something would hap-pen. Unfortunately, they were not especially impressed. Fran preached a rather long message stressing the "historical space-time baby Jesus" over and over again. While I thought it was riveting, to my parents he might as well have been from another planet!

Eventually the Schaeffers began a chapter of Children for Christ right there in their village. Amusingly, it was their children who urged them to start this work at home, calling them "frauds" for inaugurating these programs everywhere except at home. Significantly, these meetings with

---

[10] Edith Schaeffer, *Dear Family*, 257; letter dated May 1, 1977. Again, there is a poignant account of this first meeting and its significance for both men in Duriez, *Francis Schaeffer*, 76–80.
[11] Though finishing schools are rare today, in those years daughters from well-heeled families were sent to these schools and not to college, which was considered unladylike.

children, and with students as well as adults, provided a forum for the development of Fran's apologetics.

Chalet des Frênes was sold from under them, and they found a lovely place, Chalet Bijou, which in the end provided more space and comfort. There they continued their work. Fran became a keen observer of trends in Europe. The Roman Catholic Church, he was sure, was on the verge of transition. He was in Rome for the announcement about the "assumption" of the Virgin Mary (the second infallible *ex cathedra* declaration by a pope; the first being the immaculate conception of Mary in 1864) and felt sure this large body was poised for some major changes. Sure enough, in 1962–1965, Vatican II worked on the *aggiornamento* of that branch of Christianity. The winds of change within the Catholic Church, Fran believed, were not unlike the new modernism he was constantly denouncing in Protestantism. Other trends included secularization and relativism. Fran saw this in philosophy, but also in modern art, which he believed was a clear weather vane for ideas and trends sweeping across Europe.

## The Crisis

The late 1940s and early 1950s saw the seeds for many of the emphases that would characterize Fran's approach to people, to apologetics, and, most importantly, to spirituality, in his later ministry. It was during this time that a crisis hit. It was the most significant event by far, one that shaped what would really become the second phase of his life and would be the pivotal point leading to the work of L'Abri. For various reasons, at this time Fran plunged into the depths of doubt. He decided in the midst of this dark night of the soul that the only honest way forward was to rethink his entire theology and Christian commitment, even at the risk of finding it not true in the end.

Though he was occasionally prone to depression, this experience was far from merely psychological. Several factors no doubt triggered the crisis. First, his revered professor, Allan MacRae (1902–1997), who had followed McIntire out of Westminster and the Orthodox Presbyterian Church—something of a mentor to Fran—was disappointed, if not angered, by the Schaeffer's decision to move to Europe. Biographer Barry Hankins suggests that Fran needed to move beyond the sway of this tutor, who probably did not fully grasp the importance of the European theater or the work with European children. MacRae's criticisms were unsettling.[12]

Second, and more significantly, the Schaeffers had gradually become aware that their approach to various people, particularly those with whom they disagreed, had been less than loving. And they began to worry that their faith was not informed by the full reality of God's power. Fran became more and more concerned that "The Movement" was stressing doctrinal gatekeeping at the expense of love. In their defense of separation they treated people unkindly, often expending more energy on fighting fellow Christians than on countering liberalism and unbelief. Although they had been serving the Lord, they did not feel the enjoyment of the Lord that ought to accompany that service.[13]

Third, and surely not insignificantly, was Fran's encounter with Karl Barth, perhaps the most influential theologian of the twentieth century. In his concern to combat Barth's neoorthodoxy (the "new modernism"), Fran had made attempts to reach out to the great man. He and his friend James O. Buswell Jr. visited Barth in 1950.[14] Then Fran sent him a copy of a paper about neoorthodoxy[15] he was going to read for a congress in Amsterdam and requested another visit. But Barth replied within a few days with a stinging rebuke, calling Fran's theology "criminology" and raking him over the coals for his attitude. Barth refused any attempts at further conversations, arguing that conversations only occur between open-minded persons. Colin Duriez surmises that this letter might well have played a role in triggering the coming crisis. Although Fran never relented in his critique of neoorthodoxy, this admonition by Barth must have shaken him deeply.[16]

The crisis came in the early spring of 1951. As Fran would characterize things, what was basically at stake here was *reality*. For about two months he walked every day, either outdoors in the mountains or back and forth up in the hayloft of Chalet Bijou, seeking reality. He believed he had to

---

[12] Hankins, *Francis Schaeffer and the Shaping of Evangelical America*, 37.

[13] See Francis A. Schaeffer, "The Secret of Power and Enjoyment of the Lord: The Need for Both Purity and Love in the Christian Life," *The Sunday School Times*, June 16 and 23, 1951. One may receive a moving, personal insight into Schaeffer's spiritual crisis and his victory in Dennis, *Letters of Francis A. Schaeffer*, particularly part 1, "The Reawakening of Spiritual Reality."

[14] J. Oliver Buswell (1895–1977) was one of the stalwarts who founded the Orthodox Presbyterian Church, along with Machen, but then left for the Bible Presbyterian Church with McIntire and Schaeffer. Buswell did a stint as president of Wheaton College and later was dean at Covenant College, then Covenant Theological Seminary, both in St. Louis at the time.

[15] Archived in the PCA Historical Center's manuscript collection no. 29, box 134.

[16] Duriez, *Francis Schaeffer*, 101. Fran did praise Barth for his stand against the Nazis, but this did not mitigate his basic critique (*CW*, 5:189).

rethink "the whole matter of Christianity."[17] This was surely a very difficult time for the ever-supportive Edith, who knew that if Fran emerged thinking Christianity was not true, he would throw it all out. In the end, though, Fran came to believe again that the Bible was true, and that his youthful commitment to Christ had been the right move. "Finally the sun came out. I saw that my earlier decision to step from agnosticism to Bible-believing Christianity was right."[18] From then on, he remained strongly committed not only to the truth of the gospel but, most significantly, to its power. There was a once-and-for-all aspect to the work of Christ, but also a present value, leading to a present reality.

Fran did not enter this struggle looking for "true spirituality." His struggle was more basic: is Christianity true? But what emerged was inextricably tied to his conclusions about the Christian life, and these became a major theme for his speaking and writing down through the years. Truth had to be balanced with love. Fran was now a free man. He began to write poetry again and left off the dark moods he had been in. He once told me, I don't believe in the "second blessing" theology, but I think I have had one!

Edith gave birth to their fourth child, a boy named Francis August Schaeffer V, on August 3, 1952. Known for most of his early years as Franky, he now prefers to be called Frank. Not two years into his young life the poor lad began to have trouble walking and experienced muscle attacks accompanied by nausea. One of the most difficult trials the Schaeffers endured was the discovery that Franky had contracted polio. Through a series of remarkable encounters with specialists, they were able to prevent the disease from developing into its worse phases. When I first met Franky, he was twelve years old and limping, occasionally having to wear a brace. But soon he became as strong and mobile as any other young man. The story of Franky's bout with polio is movingly told in Edith's *L'Abri*.[19]

By 1953 the Schaeffers were due for a furlough. They packed up their essentials and, with the new baby, returned to the States for a period of seventeen months (May 1953 to September 1954). Fran was now inspired by his newfound spiritual reality, and a majority of his presentations focused on sanctification. These talks later were crystallized into his book *True Spirituality*.[20] One of his most powerful sermons was "Tongue of

---

[17] Edith Schaeffer, *The Tapestry*, 354–55.
[18] Francis A. Schaeffer, "Why and How I Write My Books," *Eternity Magazine*, March 24, 1973, 64, available at http://www.chaleteagle.org/library/biblio/sec-02/730300FS.htm.
[19] Edith Schaeffer, *L'Abri*, 63–71.
[20] Francis A. Schaeffer, *True Spirituality* (Wheaton, IL: Tyndale, 1972).

Fire," referring not to the charismatic experience, but to the present value of the work of Christ, accessible to anyone who asks. At the same time he denounced the sham of any sort of human counterfeit. He also spoke on subjects such as theological trends and modern art, no doubt arousing suspicion from some audiences.

At this time the Bible Presbyterian Church was going through considerable turmoil. Among the issues was the increasingly authoritarian ways of Carl McIntire.[21] The denomination finally split in two in 1956. There was the Collingswood Synod, led by McIntire, and a second Synod eventually called the Reformed Presbyterian Church, Evangelical Synod (RPCES). Fran allied himself with this latter group. The RPCES founded World Presbyterian Missions, as well as Covenant College and Covenant Theological Seminary. The RPCES eventually merged into the Presbyterian Church in America (PCA) in 1982. In the meantime, Schaeffer decided to create a new denomination serving Europe, the International Presbyterian Church. The IPC, which is still going today, was created in order to formalize the church meetings in Champéry, and also in hopes for a broader Presbyterian movement across Europe in the future. Indeed, Fran hoped that this church might somehow eclipse the work of L'Abri and become a movement that could surpass some of the roadblocks evidenced in various Reformed bodies.[22]

During this season when Fran was thinking more intentionally about the Christian life, he made a discovery that helped drive him forward. He asked Edith one day: What if God removed all the passages in the Bible referring to prayer and to the work of the Holy Spirit (not by demythologizing but by a divine editing)? What real difference would it make in their lives?[23] As we shall see, this question, and the answer, led to an increasing practice of true dependence on the Lord for their every decision. This new *reality* helped them face the difficulties of returning to Switzerland after their furlough. To get there they had to face obstacles, which included a lack of funds, and people in their mission who were critical of the Schaeffers' job description. But with determination and a fresh resolve to trust the Lord, doors were opened, and the Schaeffers did return to their beloved Chalet Bijou to carry on the work of speaking around Europe, as

[21] For an insightful discussion of McIntire's theology, some of which clearly influenced Francis Schaeffer, see, Markku Ruotsila, "Carl McIntire and the Fundamentalist Origin of the Christian Right," *Church History* 81, no. 2 (2012): 378–407.
[22] There are several active congregations of the IPC today.
[23] Edith Schaeffer, *The Tapestry*, 356.

well as receiving numerous people in their home for discussion. It was at this time that the Schaeffers saw their life's work as centering on their intentional hospitality. Fran thought they would call their work L'Abri (meaning "the shelter," taken from Ps. 91:1, as mentioned earlier).

### Eviction

Shortly after their return to Switzerland a life-changing event occurred. On February 14, 1955 (Valentine's Day!), the Schaeffers received two official letters, one ordering them to leave the canton of Valais and the other to leave the country entirely, both by March 31. The reason given was "a religious influence on the village of Champéry." Despite official religious toleration, Switzerland at the time was still quite sectarian. Apparently some of the elders of the village of Champéry had somehow convinced the authorities that this American family—Fran, Edith, and their children— was having a negative influence on the village, akin to the activities of some of the worst cults. Even though the Schaeffers had been extremely careful not to cause any undue offense, no doubt the Children for Christ ministry had been troubling to some of the mostly Roman Catholic town folk. No doubt, also, one key occurrence behind the move to expel them was that through the Schaeffers a prominent citizen of Champéry, Monsieur Georges Exhenry, head of the local electric company, had become a believer in historic Christianity, as understood by Protestant evangelicals. Monsieur Exhenry was even rebaptized and eventually was ordained as an elder in the new International Presbyterian Church. Strange but true: becoming a Protestant was still an unthinkable offense in the conservative Catholic cantons of Switzerland. It made no difference that the Schaeffers' approach bore no resemblance to the hard-sell methods of many cult leaders or evangelists.

At this point Fran decided that two strategies were open to them. The one was to contact all the authorities they could, telegram their senator, and so forth. The other was to kneel down and pray, and see what the heavenly Father would do. They chose to pray. During their prayers it occurred to Fran that they ought to contact at least one of their Protestant Swiss friends about this, so as to stave off rumors. They sent word, and their friend's response was incredulity: this wouldn't happen in Switzerland! The friend did ask to see a copy of the papers. When he saw them, to his dismay he found that there had been no mistake. But he picked up something in the fine print. They had ten days to appeal. And the very chief of the Foreign Police in Lausanne was willing to write the appeal in proper form if Fran would come down to sign it. Astonishing events followed. The American consul in Geneva urged them to go to Bern, the capital, and set forth their case to the American embassy. There they met with the senior consul, who turned out to be a high school classmate of Fran's!

The man introduced the Schaeffers to the ambassador herself. Although Switzerland was one of the only countries without a treaty with the United States regarding its citizens, and therefore any canton could by rights extradite any American without giving a reason, the ambassador found the case so unusual that she took it to the head of the National Foreign Police. One thing led to another, and as it turned out, there was one way, and one way only, that they could stay in the country: relocate to a Protestant canton. If they could do so by May 30 of that year, and own property there, then they could appeal with good hopes of staying.

The story of how they did in fact relocate in Huémoz-sur-Ollon is marvelously told by Edith in both *L'Abri* and *The Tapestry*. The Schaeffers were able to relocate across the valley, in Chalet les Mélèzes, in the tiny village of Huémoz, halfway between Ollon and Villars, in the Protestant canton of Vaud (Lausanne, where they first lived, is the capital). Edith recounts that before purchasing the chalet, which would eventually be at the center of the work of L'Abri, three hurdles, all involving money, had to be overcome. This was made more difficult for her because, while she was sure the move was right, Fran was not one hundred percent on board with the idea.

First, she asked for a clear sign that this was God's will. She prayed that $1,000 would show up miraculously. In the mail the next day came a letter with such a check, and the explanation from the donor that they had sensed an urgency about the Schaeffers' needs and had made a special trip to the mailbox during bad weather so that the letter could arrive in a timely fashion. Second, they needed eight thousand Swiss francs in order to make the down payment. This was a considerable amount of money at the time, and for the Schaeffers it was humanly impossible. Yet, counting all the gifts that came in over the next few weeks, they had 8,011 francs in hand! Third, they needed some extra funds for the closing costs. By May 30 they had everything they needed, plus about three francs (a couple of dollars) to spare!

Now, though they had no idea what the future would bring, they were living in the house that was to become "the shelter." One more obstacle needed to be overcome. The edict evicting them from Switzerland was still on the books. Their only procedural option at present was to appeal. As it happened, one of their new neighbors in Huémoz was the sister of one of the Swiss Federal Council of Seven, which is the executive branch of the government. Switzerland, radically democratic, is run by seven people, from which one member rotates into the presidency every year. Providentially, Paul Chaudet was able to check into this matter and obtain governmental permission for the Schaeffers to settle in the canton of Vaud. Their official permit came June 21!

The Schaeffers strongly sensed they were called to the kind of ministry in which they had been engaged over the previous few years. But they were increasingly uncomfortable with their sending mission. On June 5, Fran decided to resign from the Independent Board for Presbyterian Foreign Missions. This represented a critical turning point. The Schaeffers' work, they felt, was no longer strictly in line with the purposes of the IBPFM, even within the European focus that Fran had helped to define. Instead, they understood their calling to be in line with their remarkable journey. Putting it into words, they saw their purpose as "to demonstrate the existence of God in our generation."

Thus, L'Abri became a *faith mission*, that is, a work that would not ask for funds but submit everything to the Lord in prayer. Fran and Edith always explained that this was *one* way, not the *only* way, to live out one's calling. This caution cannot be stressed too strongly. But the Schaeffers' faith was a powerful testimony to those of us who were there. Furthermore, henceforth the Schaeffers no longer identified themselves with "the separated movement." Duriez concludes from this that they were now seen from the North American perspective to be simply evangelical Christians and not Reformed fundamentalists.[24]

---

[24] Duriez, *Francis Schaeffer*, 132. Fran was not reluctant to call his theology Reformed, although often qualifying it so as not to identify with hyper-Calvinism. The term *fundamentalist* has its own history and significance. Again, when pressed, even in later years Fran could call himself a fundamentalist, meaning he stood on the great fundamentals, and also that his ecclesiology favored the purity of the visible church (lists of the fundamentals vary, but usually included the plenary verbal inspiration of Scripture, the virgin birth of Jesus Christ, the substitutionary atonement, the bodily resurrection of Jesus, and the personal and visible return of Jesus). While perhaps strictly speaking the Schaeffers were no longer separatists, they strongly believed in the purity of the visible church and remained critical of pluralism and ecumenism. Fran eventually kept dual credentials, both in the International Presbyterian Church and in the Reformed Presbyterian Church, Evangelical Synod.

CHAPTER 3

# L'ABRI AND BEYOND

*I saw many people being changed at L'Abri. Many became Christian;*
*some did not. But I think that most went away with the knowledge that*
*they had been loved—with a sense of worth and a clear idea of the exis-*
*tence of God, and with the reality of communication on both the divine*
*and human level.*

MARIA WALFORD-DELLU

## Life in Huémoz

Although moving to Huémoz and leaving the Independent Board were
not altogether easy, in many ways the Schaeffers were now able to focus
entirely on the heart of their calling, the one developed in the recent years:
welcoming people from every conceivable background to their home and
commending the Christian faith to them.

As Edith recounts in *L'Abri*, people began coming up the mountain from
an astonishing array of places. Priscilla, now attending the University of
Lausanne, would bring inquiring student friends to hear her parents explain
the biblical worldview. L'Abri was truly international right from the start.
Many different Europeans would come, but also North Americans, Asians,
Africans, Latin Americans, and Australians. They heard about this place
either by word of mouth or because they had come across Fran's lectures.
Later, they might be brought there because of his publications. L'Abri developed a reputation as a place where one could go, reside for various lengths of
time, and engage in philosophical discussions about life's meaning.

Edith describes the purpose of L'Abri this way: "To show forth by demonstration, in our life and work, the existence of God."[1] This demonstration includes living on the basis of prayer. She names four petitions in particular:

1. We make our financial and material needs known to God alone, in prayer, rather than sending out pleas for money. We believe that He can put it into the minds of the people of His choice the share they should have in the work. [It should be noted that prayer requests would appear in their newsletters as well.]
2. We pray that God would bring the people of His choice to us, and keep all others away. There are no advertising leaflets, and this book is the first to be written about the work.
3. We pray that God will plan the work, and unfold His plan to us (guide us, lead us) day by day, rather than planning the future in some clever or efficient way in committee meetings.
4. We pray that God will send the workers of His choice to us, rather than pleading for workers in the usual channels.[2]

We will explore the L'Abri approach to guidance in a subsequent chapter. Suffice it to say here that while some of the details of these commitments have been slightly modified (for example, today there are websites, brochures advertising conferences, etc.), the substance has remained the same down through the years. In these early days the L'Abri family was being formed. Edith sent out some 350 letters on a regular basis. Over the years that number would grow to the thousands.[3] Edith, many of us believe, was the "hidden artist" who held L'Abri together. I am honored to have known her and will always remain grateful to her for her love and dedication.

The daily routines included discussion groups; Bible studies, both in Huémoz and in Lausanne; a fortnightly trip to Milano, where the Schaeffers' great friends the Woodsons had established a L'Abri type of work; days of prayer; Sunday worship; Children for Christ; and many, many conversations over meals, during walks, and at special times. One of my own poignant memories was walking after many meals down the Pannex Road with Fran and others. The road led to the village next door,

---

[1] Edith Schaeffer, *L'Abri* (London: Norfolk Press, 1969), 13.
[2] Ibid., 16.
[3] See Edith Schaeffer, *With Love, Edith: The L'Abri Family Letters, 1948-1960* (San Francisco: Harper & Row, 1988); and *Dear Family: The L'Abri Family Letters, 1961-1986* (San Francisco: Harper & Row, 1989).

and the small group of guests listened intently as he unfolded the beauties of the Christian faith. The breathtaking view lent support to his message. Atheists didn't have much of a chance in that setting!

Life was not easy at L'Abri. For one thing it was always cold. Fran was unusually frugal. He would guard the fireplace to make sure no one put too much wood on at one time. For another, this was the Schaeffers' home. They intentionally opened it to whoever would come, but the price they paid was high. All their wedding presents were gone after three years, and there was constant cleaning to do, dishes to wash, snow to shovel. Edith stayed up late doing chores and writing letters. Fran studied, traveled, preached, and, most of all, conversed with the growing numbers showing up at their home. He seemed tired much of the time. He often struggled with motivation just to go on, day after day. On one of his days off, I recall, after finishing an outing at the bottom of the hill, he turned to us, and then to the Lord, asking for strength to return to the fray awaiting him above. "I'm not sure I can go on," he said—but he did.

L'Abri was not run only by Fran and Edith and the immediate family. Scores of remarkable people came to help with the work, each bringing particular gifts and each shaping the community in particular ways. Donald Drew, the warm-hearted, very proper English schoolteacher added much style to the community. He also published one of the first books in the L'Abri tradition on film.[4] The Schaeffers had also taken in a disabled woman named Gracie, who helped with several aspects of the work. The remarkable African American photographer Sylvester Jacobs not only benefited greatly from the Schaeffers' work but also was able to record life at L'Abri with his exquisite photos of the place.[5] Juanita Ellwood was a tireless enabler of life at L'Abri, both in Huémoz and over the border in France. Os Guinness, with his wife, Jenny, brought his brilliant mind to bear on the development of L'Abri's apologetics. David and Jane Wells were a strong addition to the L'Abri culture. Pierre and Danièle Berthoud provided exceptional leadership in Huémoz until their move to the Reformed Seminary in Aix-en-Provence. Jerram and Vicky Barrs not only led at the British L'Abri in Greatham, but also went on to continue the Schaeffer apologetic at Covenant Seminary in St. Louis, adding their own very special literary, pastoral, and humane touch.

---

[4] Donald Drew, *Images of Man: A Critique of the Contemporary Cinema* (Downers Grove, IL: InterVarsity, 1974).
[5] Sylvester Jacobs, *Portrait of a Shelter* (Downers Grove, IL: InterVarsity, 1973).

A special gift to L'Abri was Sheila Bird, known as "Birdie." A trained social worker and psychologist, she brought a much-needed service of spiritual counseling to the more rational apologetics of the mainstream. Jane Stuart Smith, a retired opera singer, and Betty Carlson, a writer and humorist, hosted one of the liveliest chalets in Huémoz. Larry and Nancy Snyder worked in Switzerland and then went on to lead the L'Abri in Rochester, Minnesota. Dick and Mardi Keyes began in Switzerland, then went to Ealing, and finally founded the L'Abri work in Southborough, Massachusetts. Dick is perhaps one of the most creative minds that L'Abri has produced. While willingly overshadowed by the powerhouses that were Fran and Edith Schaeffer, these unsung heroes caused life on the ground to flourish. And there were so many others. And younger leaders have emerged, hosting the various branches of the work and developing in ways that would make the Schaeffers proud.[6]

## Unique Apologetics

Schaeffer continued to develop his apologetics throughout the years. Though brilliant, Fran was not an academic, at least in the strict sense. He picked up ideas here and there from essays or people he encountered. He once told me that an English journal asked him to write an article for them. He did so. But they wouldn't publish it until they had moved some of the content into footnotes to make it look more scholarly! Several accounts of his apologetics are in print. The best one to date by my lights is Bryan Follis's *Truth with Love*.[7] In order really to get a flavor for the way Schaeffer worked, though, I would recommend reading his books and listening to the many recordings of his talks.[8]

Fran's historiography was the pattern of rise and decline. The turning point in the West for him was the "line of despair," in the nineteenth century, below which philosophers and artists rejected a unified worldview and accepted the irrational. His apologetics were somewhat eclectic. He did strongly believe in the role of presuppositions at the foundation of a

---

[6] There are the inevitable purists who cannot admit that L'Abri could ever be the same without the presence of its founders. My own view is that there is still much vitality there, as people I have sent to L'Abri can testify. Naturally, some of the issues are different from the early days.

[7] Bryan A. Follis, *Truth with Love: The Apologetic of Francis A. Schaeffer* (Wheaton, IL: Crossway, 2006).

[8] We will have a brief look at some of the key books. If one is not familiar with Francis Schaeffer's written works, I would advise beginning with *Death in the City* (Downers Grove, IL: InterVarsity, 1969; reissued, Wheaton, IL: Crossway, 2002). While perhaps no exhaustive collection of recordings exists, a fairly complete resource is the L'Abri Ideas Library, http://www.labri-ideas-library.org/lecture-list.asp?s=5.

person's worldview. Although he may not have used a fully transcendental method, he had an uncanny way of identifying the contradiction between someone's basic commitments and that person's real life, and thus the impossibility of living successfully in God's world with an unbelieving philosophy.[9] As I mentioned in the personal introduction, he could engage with the smartest individual and, given time, discover that point of tension within his or her philosophical position or actual life.

Three examples of his method will have to suffice here. Bernard Berenson (1865–1959) was one of the greatest experts on Renaissance art in the twentieth century. He lived in I Tatti, the Harvard-owned villa outside of Florence. He was a truly "modern" man, Schaeffer says, and felt free to steal away Mary, the wife of Francis Costelloe. The two lived together until Francis died, whereupon they married. But the new couple decided that engaging in extramarital affairs was legitimate, and they did so rather often. When Berenson was chided for this, he replied, "You are forgetting the animal basis of our nature." At the same time he hated most modern art, finding it, among other things, bestial! Schaeffer comments, "No man like Berenson can live with his system. . . . No matter what he says he is, he still is man."[10]

A second example is from the life of Sigmund Freud (1856–1939). After describing Freud as a rationalist, one who reduced all relationships to sex, Schaeffer then points to evidence that Freud could not obviate the need for real love. In his correspondence with his fiancée about their upcoming rendezvous, Freud says, "When you come to me, little Princess, love me *irrationally*." Schaeffer adds that this is one of the saddest letters ever written, because the man is condemned by his own emotions. His being the image of God betrays him.[11]

A third example is well known in the annals of philosophy. The Scottish Enlightenment skeptic David Hume (1711–1786) denied miracles and the biblical witness on the basis that we have no proof, but only sense impressions from people in the first century. He was very close to

---

[9] The transcendental argument stemming from Immanuel Kant states that reasoning and meaning are not possible without presupposing an ultimate (transcendental) principle. Cornelius Van Til Christianized the approach to develop his "presuppositional apologetics." Among other features, presuppositionalism argues from the impossibility of the contrary. Schaeffer used this approach, but combined it with others. He thought there were objective criteria for coherency and proof, and that these should be self-evident. See Don Collett, "Van Til and the Transcendental Argument," in *Revelation and Reason: New Essays in Reformed Apologetics*, ed. K. Scott Oliphint and Lane G. Tipton (Phillipsburg, NJ: P&R, 2007), 258–78.

[10] Francis A. Schaeffer, *The God Who Is There* (Downers Grove, IL: InterVarsity, 1968), 65.

[11] Francis A. Schaeffer, *True Spirituality* (Wheaton, IL: Tyndale, 1972), 127.

pure nihilism. Yet he was famous for his inability to go all the way with his radical skepticism. In the *Treatise on Human Nature* he confesses that "neither I nor any other person was ever sincerely and constantly of [the opinion of skepticism]. . . . I dine, I play backgammon, I converse and am merry with friends."[12]

One of Fran's outstanding contributions was his unique and fresh vocabulary. Wonderfully free from technical jargon, even where traditional theology has provided sound and accurate terms, Fran coined new ones. Duriez suggests that Fran's fresh way of putting things is the perfect answer to modern art, because it defamiliarizes the familiar.[13] A few examples would include calling Christianity "true truth." Instead of talking of God's transcendence, he called him "the God who is there." Parts of Schaeffer are steeped in realism. One of his triumphant discoveries was that the risen Christ addressed Saul (soon to be Paul) on the Damascus road *in the Hebrew language*. Why should this matter? Because the reference to the Hebrew language meant that the Lord spoke concretely to Paul in a specific, space-time manner. In point of fact, the Lord may have spoken to Paul in Aramaic, which is a local variant on Hebrew, and the language Jesus likely spoke during his life on earth. But the point is the same: that this was no irrational experience of the *numinous*, but one that was accessible to reason, occurring in real history.

Fran stopped at nothing to defend the objective reality of a true religious experience over against mysticism and liberal theology. If you had been there at Calvary's cross, he said, and had rubbed your hand against it, you would have gotten a splinter![14] Instead of talking about the humanity of the person, he stressed the "mannishness of man." (He often used the generic *man*, in keeping with his times. He later explained that he meant no insult to women. And every now and then he would find a biblical reference to men and women, and pause to rejoice over God's kindness to both sexes.[15]) He said that we had "moral motions," meaning we were, like Berenson, Freud, and Hume, incapable of hiding our true ethical selves. History, he maintained, is "feminine," explaining that when we act in history, fruit is born, results happen.

During these years at the dawn of L'Abri, Schaeffer would continue to

---

[12] Francis A. Schaeffer, *Whatever Happened to the Human Race?* (Old Tappan, NJ: Revell, 1979), 133.
[13] Colin Duriez, *Francis Schaeffer: An Authentic Life* (Wheaton, IL: Crossway, 2008), 154.
[14] Schaeffer, *True Spirituality*, 34–35, 38–39.
[15] CW, 1:x; 2:350.

investigate issues with a fresh, personal drive. He was often deeply moved even as he spoke. He sometimes broke down in tears during a discussion or a sermon. His was, as Duriez puts it, an "authentic life."

## Widening Impact

L'Abri expanded in many ways. As early as 1956 Hans and Anky Rookmaaker came down to Switzerland with their family. Soon thereafter, the Dutch branch was inaugurated. Similarly, the English L'Abri began in 1964, to be headed by Ranald and Susan (Schaeffer) Macaulay. Eventually, this extraordinary work of L'Abri, whether in Huémoz or elsewhere, would attract notice, including from the media. In 1960 *Time* magazine published an article about it entitled "Mission to the Intellectuals." It was that, but it was so much more. L'Abri was reaching people who would not necessarily have been drawn to a typical evangelistic campaign.[16]

Stories of how people got to L'Abri could be multiplied. Marc Mailloux was an aspiring Buddhist mystic, traveling from Europe to India and to other places in Asia, when he met an American hippie woman on a beach in Corfu who explained L'Abri as "a place to crash for a few days—especially if you're low on funds; beautiful scenery and pretty good vibes, even if most of the folks there are into a religious trip."[17] Helen Cooper was an interpreter for the United Nations and had numerous objections to the Christian faith, including the Bible's cruelty to animals (because of animal sacrifices in the Old Testament). She went up to Huémoz on a dare from a friend she had met at the University of Geneva. Fran spent hours with her, finally challenging her about the leather shoes she was wearing! Paul, Jim, and another Jim were southerners, GIs stationed in Germany, and had heard about L'Abri through the military grapevine. Over the years, stories such as these would number in the thousands.

By the time I arrived at L'Abri in 1964, the community included five chalets in addition to Les Mélèzes. Each of them was run by families who were hosts to the visitors and students who showed up. Along with most of the men I was housed in Chalet Bethany, hosted by Joe and Linette Martin. Joe was my first "tutor in Christ." He would patiently answer my questions,

---

[16] An insightful point made by Michael Hamilton, "The Dissatisfaction of Francis Schaeffer," *Christianity Today*, March 3, 1997, 30. He amusingly says that one could no more imagine Schaeffer playing golf with the rich and famous (a legitimate activity for Billy Graham) than picture Mother Teresa shopping for furs in I. Magnin!

[17] Marc Mailloux, *Discovery on the Katmandu Trail* (Columbus, GA: Quill, 1978), 5.

not always by giving me the Christian response but by showing me where to find it. I will be eternally grateful for this patient and kind man's attentiveness to this young student, once quite lost but now secure in his faith. When my Barbara came to L'Abri, she was lodged with the women at Chalet Beau Site, owned in part by Madame Chaudet, whose brother helped procure the Schaeffer's residency permit. The hosts were newlyweds, David and Jane Wells, a dedicated family who practiced matchless hospitality. The Wellses remain our good friends to this day. Barbara remembers one evening being told, in good L'Abri fashion, to take the mattress off her bed and sleep on the box springs in order to accommodate one more unannounced guest!

Beau Site was also the place where we studied. L'Abri had received theological books from various donors, and they had acquired a set of tape recorders so that recorded lectures could be studied and digested. L'Abri gave the name Farel House to the study center, in memory of the fiery French Reformer William Farel (1489–1565), who evangelized much of francophone Switzerland in the sixteenth century. Ironically, at first, Fran rejected the tape recorder, deeming it mechanical and artificial. Then one day someone hid a microphone in a plant, and the bootlegged recording was used to spread the L'Abri message. When Fran found out, he was furious. But he soon came to see the great advantage of multiplying his audience. This was distance learning before its time!

A typical day at L'Abri consisted of an early rise, then breakfast, then four hours of study in the morning, followed by an extended lunch, and then four hours of physical work around the community. Most evenings we had dinner, followed by a long walk, and then, at least twice a week, a lecture on a given topic. The physical work we were assigned was not meant to be cheap labor, but was considered as much of a learning experience as the intellectual study. Whenever I go back, I always head over to a stone wall I built just below the village—I left my mark there, even as the place left its mark on me!

A magnificent chapel was built in the fall of 1964, which meant worship services could be held in a church building. Though we were no longer in a cozy living room, efforts were made to sustain the feeling of family worship. Babies gurgled. Most of us sat on the floor. Sitting in the back, Edith illustrated the sermons for the children. Things were rather informal. No one except Fran wore a necktie. (Preaching was considered serious business—sermons were long, thoughtful, and carefully constructed, and you dressed accordingly!) The astonishing view of the mountains to the south meant that the preacher had to be very good to hold everyone's attention! The church was given an exquisite tracker-action Flentrop organ from the famous company in Zaandam, Holland. Eventually Farel House was moved into the lower story of the chapel. So the International Presbyterian Church had a place to worship and to meet for business, which helped make it clear that L'Abri and the church were not the same thing. Many special events—including weddings, baptisms, and funerals, as well as concerts and various lectures—were held in that beautiful building.

The various emphases and themes that characterized L'Abri came out of the Schaeffers' convictions about biblical Christianity, but also from their unique experiences. As he interacted with the culture of the 1960s, Fran in a way came into his own. He was especially effective and credible responding to those times. Surely the Schaeffers were called "for such a time as this" (Est. 4:14). Having lived my own defining years in that tumultuous period, I witnessed firsthand the unsettling sea change that was occurring. Confusing, refreshing, dangerous, creative—that decade was unlike any other.[18] Often, our parents, coming from the "greatest generation," having known the depression and then the war, were unable to give any good reasons for hard work or morality. Were it not for the Schaeffers, many of us wonder where we might be today.

Among the issues that Fran addressed in that day was the Berkeley Free Speech movement beginning in 1964. Along with the hippie phenomenon and the increasing fascination with hallucinogenic drugs, the Free Speech movement developed spontaneously, until it morphed into the New Left, led by Herbert Marcuse. For Schaeffer the whole thing represented a quest for meaning, and he spent hours explaining to puzzled adults that such a quest was to be expected because they had not provided a basis for meaning and value. Similarly, Fran's interest in popular culture opened many doors for him. For a conservative pastor, he was surprisingly conversant with the music of Bob Dylan, the Jefferson Airplane, and the Beatles, as well as the novels of Terry Southern and Ken Kesey.

---

[18] The 1960s are one of the most widely analyzed decades in history. For salient accounts, see Todd Gitlin, *The Sixties: Years of Hope, Days of Rage* (New York: Bantam, 1993); Os Guinness, *The Dust of Death: A Critique of the Establishment and the Counter Culture and the Proposal for a Third Way* (Downers Grove, IL: InterVarsity, 1973).

As mentioned earlier, Fran came to the States several times during these years. He lectured at secular universities such as Harvard and Yale, but also at Christian colleges such as Wheaton and Westmont. In September 1965 he spoke at Wheaton's Spiritual Emphasis Week. By then Fran had crystallized his basic apologetics into a lecture series entitled "Speaking Historic Christianity into the Twentieth-Century World." A friend of mine who was there at the time told me that attendance was required, and the series on spiritual emphasis was often led by sincere missionaries or other evangelical personalities who did not know how to attract the interest of the students. For them it was all too predictable, and if you looked closely, you would see many students paging through *Time* magazine or the like. When Fran started talking about the "line of despair" and how films by Ingmar Bergman and Federico Fellini powerfully portrayed existentialism, the magazines dropped and the astonished students listened to life-changing content. Neither students nor faculty had ever heard anything remotely like this. Here was the evangelical Francis Schaeffer, dressed in his Swiss hiking britches and speaking with his Germantown drawl, telling them about how to read the European avant-garde film culture and other evidences of the twentieth-century ethos.

Wheaton actually printed up these lectures, and when Fran saw the resulting booklet, he became persuaded that he ought to commit this material to book form. The result was *The God Who Is There* (actually his second book). He had published a few articles, as well as homegrown texts, such as *Basic Bible Studies* (which later became *25 Basic Bible Studies*), and his *Empire Builders for Boys* and *Empire Builders for Girls*. But now he would begin a career as the author of many books.

His first commercially published book was *Escape from Reason* (1968), a journey through Western history featuring various dichotomies, in a way reminiscent of Herman Dooyeweerd's *The Roots of Western Culture*.[19] As were most of his books, this one was the result of a series of lectures he gave (in this case, in Great Britain). It was followed by *The God Who Is There* (1968), expanding on the Wheaton lectures, in which he set forth his basic apologetics. The diversity of his publications is astonishing. His series on the book of Jeremiah, *Death in the City* (1969), is less a commentary on

---

[19] Toronto: Wedge, 1979. Duriez looks closely at the relation of these two authors in *Francis Schaeffer*, 172–75, and concludes that Schaeffer was influenced by the family of thinkers that includes the Amsterdam philosophers, such as Dooyeweerd, as well as Van Til, even though when asked directly, Schaeffer was vague about how that influence may have happened.

the Old Testament prophet than a sweeping defense of the combination of truth and love needed for apologetics to a post-Christian world. One of his most original books is a treatise on ecology, *Pollution and the Death of Man* (1970), written well before evangelicals became serious about the environment.

The books kept pouring forth. *True Spirituality* (1971), which will be basic to our reflections later on, builds on the sermon series he gave several times. Schaeffer would add a third volume of basic apologetics to accompany the first two, *He Is There and He Is Not Silent* (1972). The three make up a sort of trilogy on the issue of knowledge.[20] Over the next few years Francis Schaeffer would publish some twenty-two books or booklets, selling literally in the millions of copies in over twenty-five languages. In many ways Schaeffer and InterVarsity Press were good for each other. Schaeffer's books injected some new life into the venerable company. At the same time, InterVarsity Press gave him a platform and credibility he might not have gained otherwise. And, as mentioned, Crossway Books published his complete works in 1982 (including all but his last one).

Edith became a prolific author in her own right, with some eight titles as well as the family letters to her name. Her books were often (though not exclusively) about the domestic side of life at L'Abri. A book that spoke to many of us at the time is *What Is a Family?* (1975). One of her most beautifully crafted books is *Forever Music* (1986), using the metaphor of the piano to describe the Christian life. Among her more poignant books is *Affliction* (1978), including chapters titled "Why, Why, Why?" and "Cracked Teapots," in which she describes, sometimes excruciatingly, how we must suffer in the Christian life, but how God uses this for good, even though we may not see it at the time. She also wrote books on the Scriptures, such as *Christianity Is Jewish* (1977), a defense of the Hebrew roots of the Christian faith, along with her sometimes peculiar views on eschatology.

These books by Fran and Edith were and are greatly influential. Still today I often meet people who tell me that Francis Schaeffer changed their lives because of his writings, even though they never met him or went to L'Abri. One of the most common testimonies is from Christians who had never known it was legitimate to think about culture, or even to think at all.

---

[20] Francis A. Schaeffer, *The Francis A. Schaeffer Trilogy: The Three Essential Books in One Volume* (Wheaton, IL: Crossway, 1990). A study guide to the three volumes, *Introduction to Francis Schaeffer: Study Guide to a Trilogy*, was published by InterVarsity in 1977.

One of the most unusual endeavors the Schaeffers engaged in was filmmaking. I mentioned in the first chapter my own involvement in one of the films. On the whole, evangelical films at the time were predictable and simplistic. Again, Fran had to be persuaded to go into this medium. As mentioned above, the genesis of his first film, *How Should We Then Live?*, was partly due to Franky's persuasive powers. As we have seen, he and others built on Fran's concern that the BBC/PBS series *Civilisation*, featuring Kenneth Clark,[21] was unfair to many episodes in history, especially the Reformation. Once Fran was persuaded to make the film, a team of researchers was gathered, a script was drafted, and then came the shooting, done literally all over the world. Fran had been working on a massive history of the West since 1974, but now it could come together in a single oeuvre.

The book and the film are elaborately furnished with quotes and take us to locations and artwork from the ancient Greeks down to the present. The history follows a "rise and decline" story line.[22] Beginning with Rome, the episodes show how any attempt to build a government and a culture on the oppressive control of the Caesars (or any other tyrant) combined with the indifference of the population to things that matter for their humanity is doomed to fail. In the Middle Ages the process of Christianization led to an extraordinary synthesis between church and society, but one that ultimately could not stand. The Renaissance was an attempt to reassert the glory of mankind. Then came the Reformation, clearly Fran's favorite, a place where biblical Christianity was able to take root and bring a degree of freedom and humanity never before known.

The modern decline begins at the Enlightenment and then goes through the process leading to the line of despair and to breakdowns of all kinds. All of this is lavishly illustrated.[23] At the more technical level, while

---

[21] It first aired on the BBC in 1969 and then on PBS in the United States in 1970.

[22] This is not unlike Otto Spengler's "seasonal" approach in his two-volume *Decline of the West* (1918, 1923), albeit without such categories as Spengler's distinction between culture and civilization. Schaeffer directly mentions Edward Gibbon's *Decline and Fall of the Roman Empire* (1776–1788) and suggests that today we are experiencing the same symptoms as Rome in its deterioration (*How Should We Then Live?* [Old Tappan, NJ: Revell, 1976], 227). Several places in the film and elsewhere he says that he expects things to get far worse. For example, in "Ash Heap Lives" (a sermon and chapter in *No Little People*), he declares that "the next two to five decades will make the last few years look like child's play" (*CW*, 3:181). Schaeffer nowhere articulates a particular theory of culture. At times he sounds close to the realist philosopher Charles S. Peirce (1839–1914); at others he is simply informal and talks about "cultural life," "the general culture," "cultural consensus," and the like.

[23] Art historians might struggle with Schaeffer's sometimes reductionist approach, which involves saying, in effect, "this trend is biblical; that one has real beauty but is humanistic; this piece of music lacks resolution," and so forth. But what saves this endeavor from being a simple Manichean white-hats-versus-black-hats list of artists is Fran's obvious passion for many of the works themselves, stemming from his deep personal acquaintance with them over the years.

it represented a certain response to Kenneth Clark, it lacked the polished professionalism of the BBC/PBS series and indeed could never have hoped to make it to public television. Frank Schaeffer rather cynically reports that they enjoyed the martyrdom of being ignored by the media.[24] In reality I think it was a great disappointment to Fran, although no doubt he lacked the objectivity to see the film's shortcomings. Perhaps its greatest virtue was simply that it existed. Nothing like this had ever been attempted by an evangelical.

One effect of working on this film was a fairly radical change in the Schaeffers' relation to L'Abri. Edith recounts the difficulty of their days as filmmakers. From a personal standpoint it meant submitting to the exigencies of film production: travel, early mornings, makeup, script memorization, continuity editing, and so on. By comparison, L'Abri was "normal."[25] Beginning in 1975 and extending well into 1977, the shooting and then the numerous seminars across North America and Europe meant the Schaeffers were not nearly as present in Huémoz as they had been. In the earlier days one could frequent L'Abri and be practically guaranteed to see Fran or Edith, and usually engage in personal discussion with one of them. Now, however, the Schaeffers moved to a little chalet up the hill from Huémoz and could only be seen by appointment when they were in residence. They did all they could to keep the spirit of L'Abri the same, but the place had to change, and not all of the change was a bad thing.

Several bitter blows greeted them in the year of these tours. In 1977 Edith's father, George Seville, died at age 101. Hans Rookmaaker died unexpectedly at the age of fifty-five, leaving many projects half finished and ending a lifelong friendship. A third blow, not from a death, but still difficult, was a fire, which burned down the chapel, Farel House and all. Eventually, and at great cost, the chapel and the Flentrop organ were rebuilt. But these were very hard times.

### Into Public Policy

Francis Schaeffer grew increasingly concerned for public policy and law. With considerable persuasion by Franky, the final episode of *How Should We Then Live?* commented on the critical US Supreme Court decision of

---

[24] Frank Schaeffer, *Crazy for God: How I Grew Up as One of the Elect, Helped Found the Religious Right, and Lived to Take All (or Almost All) of It Back* (New York: Carroll & Graf, 2007), 254.
[25] Edith Schaeffer, *Dear Family*, 240–41.

January 22, 1973, known as *Roe v. Wade*. In the event, the court decided
7–2 that a woman's "right to privacy" meant she could determine the fate
of her unborn child without government interference in the first trimester of her pregnancy, and then in the second trimester she could abort if
there were no health issue. Only in the third trimester does the government have vested interest in the well-being of the unborn.[26] Schaeffer, who
had always opposed abortion on demand, called this a case of an "arbitrary absolute" being exercised by the state. He argues in the chapter "Our
Society" that the state has stripped the unborn of the status of person-
hood. Roe v. Wade is simply medically invalid, let alone legally problem-
atic. He compares this monumental error to the arbitrary declaration until
the Civil War that black people were not fully human.[27]

Schaeffer argues that a society in which a Christian consensus about
right and wrong is gone has only two alternatives open to it. The first is
hedonism, living by whatever feels good. Hedonism falls apart on its own
grounds, since there is no way to resolve a clash of pleasure seekers each
wanting his own way. The second is the rule of a 51 percent vote. Law and
morals work on the basis of averages in this case, so that there is nothing to prevent a Hitler, who won elections "legitimately," from rising to
power and destroying society. Being right becomes a matter of statistics.
Fran makes a stark diagnosis: "If there are no absolutes by which to judge
society, then society is absolute."[28] The potential tyrants are likely to be
intellectuals, Schaeffer avers, or at least part of the "technological elite."
From there he goes on to posit various possible elite rulers, none of them
friendly to traditional biblical religion.

Fran would create a second film series, together with his old friend Dr.
C. Everett Koop, who had treated Franky in the early stages of his polio,
and who eventually became surgeon general under President Ronald
Reagan. Koop had always been an opponent of therapeutic abortion, as
well as infanticide and euthanasia, and had written a powerful treatise on
life and death issues, *The Right to Live and the Right to Die* (1976). Unlike
the first series, which was entirely funded by Billy Zeoli's gospel films,
this new one was made by the new Franky Schaeffer V Productions and
funded by a number of sources from the emerging Moral Majority. Again,

---

[26] Functionally this entailed abortion on demand in all three trimesters, given the concurrent opinion of
*Doe v. Bolton* with its subjective interpretation of "health" as including emotions, family, psychology, etc.
[27] Schaeffer, *How Should We Then Live?*, 223.
[28] Ibid., 224.

there was a book to accompany the movie. The film, *Whatever Happened to the Human Race?*, was a thoughtful appeal for human life in the face of an increasing pressure to downplay the significance of the unborn and the elderly.

Francis Schaeffer, it should be mentioned, became increasingly identified with America's Religious Right. Judgments are difficult to make here, at least for me. One infamous article in the German newsweekly *Der Spiegel* suggested Fran was "the philosopher of the Moral Majority," even calling him "an Ayatollah of the Scriptures."[29] This is surely not accurate. Plainly, he did have a relationship, even an influence on the Religious Right. And it is certainly true that Frank Schaeffer had a role in persuading his father to become allied with some of this group. But I find the story line in *Crazy for God* hard to accept as a whole. Frank makes it appear as though he were his dad's equal, and that they partnered together in promoting this much more politicized version of the Christian worldview. He claims that he was the ultimate influence in getting Fran into the limelight and connected with Jerry Falwell, Pat Robertson, D. James Kennedy, and the like. He also maintains that his dad did not particularly like most of these new allies and yet allowed himself to be used by them in his desperation to change American culture. Frank explains that all of this was a huge mistake on his part.[30]

To be sure, then, Frank played some part in galvanizing the Religious Right and involving his father. But Fran had always been concerned about tyranny and about the fate of a culture that was callous about human life. He had always been concerned to live a simple life and depend directly on the Lord, rather than submit to programs and to the machinations of socialism. While I was at L'Abri, he gave a lecture on Rousas J. Rushdoony (1916–2001), the theonomist, and rather sided with his conservative assessment of the American Constitution. So, while it did seem to many of us that Fran was at his peak in the 1960s, when L'Abri was responding so creatively to the cries of our generation, these political themes were not entirely absent in those days, although perhaps they were more subsumed under Fran's general critique of culture than later.

---

[29] *Der Spiegel*, May 16, 1983, 192–99.
[30] The subtitle of his controversial book is revealing—*How I Grew Up as One of the Elect, Helped Found the Religious Right, and Lived to Take All (or Almost All) of It Back*. Several helpful reviews are available. The most sharply critical is Os Guinness, "Fathers and Sons," *Books and Culture* 14, no. 2 (March/April 2008): 32–33. I very much appreciated the review by Gregory Reynolds, "Too Frank by Half: What Love Should Have Covered," *Ordained Servant Online*, available at http://www.opc.org/os.html?article_id=132.

Out of concern, I did discuss his allegiances with the Religious Right openly with him. He was predictably articulate in explaining that he could be "cobelligerent" with all kinds of people without being their "allies."[31] And even though he admired the Moral Majority for its stand on freedom and the rule of law, Schaeffer was not in any way a patsy to the leaders of the evangelical right.[32] In *A Christian Manifesto* (1981) he sets forth in some detail his approach to American politics, as we shall see. He saw the "Reagan revolution" as a possible window of opportunity for Christians who were pro-life. But he carefully warned that "we should not wrap Christianity in our national flag."[33]

As mentioned earlier, Fran had already engaged in a lively debate with historians Mark Noll and George Marsden over the degree to which the Founding Fathers of America were self-consciously Christian.[34] Noll was troubled by Fran's historiography about the Founding Fathers, believing the situation to be far more complex than to see a "Christian consensus" across the board. Yet Schaeffer was not claiming the older days were better, in the manner of a D. James Kennedy. Throughout he was concerned to show that the Christian faith should not be *conservative* but *revolutionary*. A conservative is just part of the status quo, whereas revolutionaries are a minority that must buck the tide.[35]

Toward the end of *A Christian Manifesto*, Fran allows for Christians to disobey, but only when the state requires something that violates their conscience and when there is no other option. On civil disobedience, he generally sides with the magisterial Reformers (Luther, Zwingli, Calvin), who advocated patience and a willingness to die for one's faith, and who allowed violent resistance only as a last resort, and then only when authorized by a political entity, and never as vigilante justice. He makes several suggestions for putting government under pressure to do the right thing.

---

[31] *CW*, 4:30.

[32] *CW*, 5:450.

[33] *CW*, 5:485–86. He says elsewhere that "patriotic loyalty must *not* be identified with Christianity" (*CW*, 4:71).

[34] To arrive at a proper understanding of the relation of Schaeffer's Christian convictions to the emergence of the Christian Right would require probing deeply into American religious history. Not only the more recent history since the 1970s, but also the larger background, beginning at least with the Civil War, feeds into the mentalities that could produce a Francis Schaeffer. See Daymon A. Johnson, "Francis A. Schaeffer: An Analysis of His Religious, Social, and Political Influence on the New Christian Right" (MA thesis, California State University, 1990). Two helpful recent studies are Daniel K. Williams, *God's Own Party: The Making of the Christian Right* (New York: Oxford University Press, 2010); and Darren Dochuk, *From Bible Belt to Sunbelt: Plain-Folk Religion, Grassroots Politics, and the Rise of Evangelical Conservatism* (New York: W. W. Norton, 2010).

[35] *CW*, 4:70.

He stops short of calling Christians to revolt.[36] Perhaps some of his follow-ers did not fully hear his cautions.

Fran has been accused, even by close associates and family, of hav-ing returned later in life to the earlier battles over biblical interpretation and church separation. It is true that he often spoke and wrote on issues such as biblical inerrancy and the purity of the church in these days. But those subjects had never been muted, anymore than his political stand, even during the heyday of L'Abri in the 1960s. More than ever, in his later days he insisted that church separation, if necessary, always be conducted with love and forbearance.

## The Last Years

During the shooting of *Whatever Happened to the Human Race?*, Edith noticed that Fran had lost a considerable amount of weight. A visit in 1978 to the Mayo Clinic in Rochester, Minnesota, found him to have grown a large tumor caused by lymphoma. The tumor was malignant, and che-motherapy commenced. He went into remission for several months, and then the cancer returned. More chemotherapy followed. This affliction did not prevent him from working very hard. In the midst of it all, the Schaeffers began a new L'Abri in Rochester. Although their home remained in Switzerland, they continued to do L'Abri work in Rochester, whether in large conferences or in the traditional small groups in the living room. That work continues to flourish today.

Fran laughed when anyone suggested he might retire. He wrote one more book, centering on the issue of biblical inerrancy, *The Great Evangelical Disaster* (1984). Again, some argued that here was more evi-dence that he was returning to his original separatism and that perhaps he was getting a bit desperate, knowing his time was short. He was frustrated at not seeing change occur. But my own view is that his basic approach to the Scriptures and its interface with history and scientific data was no dif-ferent in this last book from what it had been all along.

Fran battled for six years with cancer. On his very last public tour,

---

[36] Schaeffer asks, "What does all this mean in practice for us today? I must say, I really am not sure all that it means to us in practice at this moment" (*A Christian Manifesto*, in *CW*, 5:493). Perhaps some of the uncertainty arises because he had also praised Jonathan Blanchard, founder of Wheaton College, and Charles Finney, president of Oberlin College, for calling for civil disobedience "if a law is wrong" (*CW*, 5:453). He labels the actions of the Founding Fathers as a bottom-line action of civil disobedience (*CW*, 5:490).

in 1984, he lectured in thirteen different cities on the dangers of evangelical accommodation. He was so weak he often had to be taken to the next location on a stretcher. Throughout his ministry, and now more than ever, Fran considered death to be abnormal. He often remarked after contracting cancer that he was thankful for a theology that fully believed in aggressive medical treatment, not for a moment succumbing to the "grim reaper." Ultimately, however, his hope was in the resurrection of the dead. Those who were with him at his deathbed, mostly family, attest to his fighting spirit right to the end. Even in his semi-comatose dreams he worried about the next speaking engagement, not forgetting his notes, and, most of all, whether he had gotten the message out faithfully. He certainly had. He departed this world on May 15, 1984, a world that would not see the likes of him again.

PART 2

# TRUE SPIRITUALITY

CHAPTER 4

# FUNDAMENTALS

*If our doctrine be true, and our lives be wrong, how terrible is our sin!*
*For then we have brought despite upon the truth itself.*

J. GRESHAM MACHEN

## The Genesis

Having looked briefly at the man and his times, we may now move to a discussion of Francis Schaeffer's views on the Christian life. The present chapter will examine some of the fundamentals that shape the foundation for his views. Then in the two subsequent chapters we will take a close look at his book *True Spirituality*. After that we will discuss his views on prayer and guidance, suffering, the church, and cultural engagement.

It is commonly acknowledged, and corroborated by the man himself, that Francis Schaeffer's most fruitful years, particularly in the work of L'Abri, resulted from the spiritual crisis he went through in 1951–1952, briefly described above. As he states in the preface to *True Spirituality*, it all centered on the problem of *reality*. Here is his own account of that crisis and its result:

> I had become a Christian from agnosticism many years before [the crisis]. After that I had become a pastor for ten years in the United States, and then for several years my wife Edith and I had been working in Europe. During this time I felt a strong burden to stand for the historical [*sic*] Christian position, and for the purity of the visible church.

Gradually, however, a problem came to me—the problem of reality. This had two parts: first, it seemed to me that among many of those who held the orthodox position, one saw little reality in the things that the Bible so clearly says should be the result of Christianity. Second, it gradually grew on me that my own reality was less than it had been in the early days after I had become a Christian. I realized that in honesty I had to go back and rethink my whole position.[1]

He goes on to describe the process, which we looked at in chapter 2 above, of his reexamination of the whole Christian view of life and the world. Fran walked and walked, and looked closely at what the Bible claimed. He also looked honestly into his own motives for receiving the gospel message.

Although I often heard Fran refer to this experience, few details were revealed. Perhaps it is best to leave it a private matter. Knowing Fran's temperament, we can only guess that it was a very difficult passage, full of risk. Had he decided that the gospel was not true, he would most certainly have thrown all of the Christian religion out. What else he might have done is disquieting to think about. Edith, only briefly, though poignantly, describes this "hayloft" experience of Fran's in *The Tapestry*. She quotes him as saying:

Edith, I really feel torn to pieces by the lack of reality, the lack of seeing the results the Bible talks about, which should be seen in the Lord's people. I'm not only talking about people I'm working with in "The Movement," but I'm not satisfied with myself. It seems that the only honest thing to do is to rethink, reexamine the whole matter of Christianity. Is it true? I need to go back to my agnosticism and start at the beginning.[2]

She compares this experience to the Slough of Despond in John Bunyan's *Pilgrim's Progress*. And then she moves on to say that this was all very private, and that she needed wisdom to know when to ask questions and when to remain silent. In the end, however, Fran emerged absolutely certain that God is "there," that the Bible is true, and that there can be reality in the Christian life. And the thousands of people he helped because he himself had blazed a difficult trail made it all worthwhile. He emerged from this long dark period full of hope and conviction. It was all true after all! As he explains, this is the real source of L'Abri. The apologetic answers

---

[1] CW, 3:195.
[2] Edith Schaeffer, *The Tapestry: The Life and Times of Francis and Edith Schaeffer* (Waco, TX: Word, 1981), 354–55.

are important, but knowing the present value of Christ's work of redemption is paramount.

One matter is clear. This crisis sent Fran to look into the present meaning of the finished work of Christ for our lives in a way he had never done before. Schaeffer's views on spirituality were developed throughout his life, but this experience represents a significant milestone.

### Gospel Basics

Unlike some who have had something like a second experience of the grace of God in their lives, Fran never attempted to "canonize" it, to make the experience a norm and standard for everyone. Occasionally, when addressing the issue of sanctification, he says things such as, "Sanctification is a process, not an act, and yet there are often one or more crises along the way as a Christian gains new knowledge of the meaning and the work of Christ in his present life and as he begins to act on that knowledge."[3] But this never means either a normative experience or a qualitative leap that puts someone on a higher plane.

Right at the beginning of *True Spirituality* he makes the simple but fundamental point that there is no Christian life at all unless one is a Christian. "The first point which we must make is that it is impossible even to begin living the Christian life, or to know anything of true spirituality, before one is a Christian."[4] He goes on to explain that the only way to become a Christian is not through a religious experience, but "by accepting Christ as Savior." Whether one is a highly educated or complicated person or a simpler one, the initial step is the same without exception. Schaeffer supports the claim by quoting Jesus's "exclusive word," which is, "No man cometh unto the Father but by me" (John 14:6).[5]

What are those fundamentals for Schaeffer? He briefly outlines them in the next few paragraphs of *True Spirituality*. To begin with, everyone is separated from God by true moral guilt. Here and throughout his writings, Schaeffer makes a basic distinction between true moral guilt and guilt feelings, which are not at all the same. He was ever pleading for an objective response to a real world. While it is possible to overreact and become

---

[3] *CW*, 4:177.
[4] *CW*, 3:199.
[5] *CW*, 3:199. Schaeffer used the King James Version in most of his writings, although he had nothing against newer translations. Similarly, his prayers used *Thee* and *Thou*, even though he was fine with the vernacular. Occasionally I will use the ESV when it is helpful to the modern reader.

intellectualistic about matters of faith, he saw his main mission as the defense of *true truth*. This unique expression is telling. Schaeffer's intention was to defend the whole notion of truth to the core. What appears as a redundancy is for him a way to insist that truth is paramount. We have all sinned before a holy and just God, not by mistake but intentionally.

Second, only the substitutionary atonement of Jesus Christ, his death in space and in time, can remedy this condition. Our true guilt can be removed only on the basis of the finished work of Christ "plus nothing on our part" (again, a constant theme in his writings).[6] "When we thus come, believing God, the Bible says we are declared justified by God; the guilt is gone, and we are returned to fellowship with God—the very thing for which we were created in the first place."

Third, Schaeffer explains the nature of faith. It is not a "Kierkegaardian" leap in the dark, but rather a lifting of the "empty hands of faith" in order to accept the finished work of Christ on the cross in history.[7]

At L'Abri, when someone expressed interest in or commitment to the gospel, before acknowledging that person to be a Christian, Schaeffer would go over four questions:

1. Do you believe that God exists and that he is a personal God, and that Jesus Christ is God—remembering that we are not talking of the *word* or *idea* god, but of the infinite-personal God who is there?

2. Do you acknowledge that you are guilty in the presence of God— remembering that we are not talking about guilt feelings, but true moral guilt?

3. Do you believe that Jesus Christ died in space and time, in history, on the cross, and that when He died His substitutional [sic] work of bearing God's punishment against sin was fully accomplished and complete?

4. On the basis of God's promises in His written communication to us, the Bible, do you (or have you) cast yourself on this Christ as your personal Savior—not trusting in anything you yourself have ever done or ever will do?[8]

---

[6] *CW*, 3:200.

[7] *CW*, 3:200. Schaeffer's interpretation of Søren Kierkegaard's fideism has been disputed. See, for example, Ronald W. Ruegsegger, "Schaeffer on Philosophy," in *Reflections on Francis Schaeffer*, ed. Ronald W. Ruegsegger (Grand Rapids: Zondervan, 1986), 118–20. It is quite legitimate to recognize Kierkegaard as a defender of orthodoxy; yet he was sufficiently ambiguous that we can well understand those who would view his commitment to the "absurd" as paving the way to existentialism. One could say that, at best, Kierkegaard left himself open to the charge.

[8] *CW*, 1:147.

**Truth's Authority**

These basics of the gospel are found throughout his writings. And it is clear that the Christian worldview includes more than the gospel story. Schaeffer would often say that truth comes before the matter of salvation. What is that truth? Francis Schaeffer was an evangelical through and through. Because he was a historic protestant, Schaeffer's ultimate court of appeal was the Bible. It gives us final and sufficient knowledge because it alone, not the church or natural theology, is our authority.[9] The Bible is God's inerrant word.[10] In the article "What Difference Does Inerrancy Make?" (March 1982), Schaeffer warns against the strand in contemporary evangelicalism that has a weakened view of Scripture.[11] The article centers on the ethical issues of the day, particularly abortion. When the Bible is not considered inerrant, what gets lost is our ability to stand against the surrounding culture, which is ever changing and fallen.[12] Indeed, the culture begins to judge the Bible, not the other way around. In this same article, and throughout his work, Schaeffer reminds us that it is one thing to believe correctly about the Bible's authority, but it is another, and equally important, to live according to the Bible.

Schaeffer defends the Bible's authority all through his work. His central apologetic concern is that we not dichotomize the Bible's message as being true only in the religious sphere while fallible in the realms where science and history can verify its claims. The "religious" truth of the Bible is of the same nature as the truth about everyday life. If the Bible affirms the physical resurrection of Jesus, then his body will never be found where he was buried. Ultimately the Hebrew and biblical view grounds the truth in the character of God, who reveals himself in both the creation and special revelation.[13]

Although Schaeffer did not explore the science of biblical hermeneutics in any depth, he did believe in the analogy of Scripture as taught by the Reformers. That is, one portion of Scripture can explain another, because the Bible is one book. Thus, in his *Basic Bible Studies* he declares that "because one of the wonderful things about the Bible is its unity,

---

[9] *CW*, 1:218.
[10] *CW*, 1:86–89; 2:23, etc.
[11] "What Difference Does Inerrancy Make?," appendix B to *The Church at the End of the Twentieth Century*, in *CW*, 4:103–10.
[12] *CW*, 4:106.
[13] *CW*, 5:391–92.

nit.""[14] Both in
his preaching and in extended scripturally based studies, Schaeffer uses
a thematic approach rather than a biblical-theological approach. That is,
he draws on many portions of Scripture, using something like a cumulative effect, in order to derive a doctrine or make a point, rather than taking
a specific text both in its original horizon and then in its relation to the
historical unfolding of redemptive history, culminating in Christ.[15] Such
a "proof-text method," as the older approach is sometimes known, is not
wrong, since the Bible does have a fundamental unity within its diversity.
Indeed, Schaeffer was thoroughly committed to the unity of the Scriptures.
In his personal devotions he read something like four chapters of the Old
Testament and one chapter from the New Testament every day. But such
a focus on the unity of the Bible may deprive one of the richness of a particular portion's literary structure, or of the place of a revelation within a
specific season in the flow of redemptive history. It may also minimize the
human side of biblical revelation. While Schaeffer certainly recognized the
human factor in the Bible, it was not his primary interest.

Of course, he acknowledged the progressive nature of redemptive history in the broadest sense, that is, the relation of the old covenant to the
new.[16] But he resisted such things as attributing typology to Old Testament
figures unless the Bible explicitly allows it. For example, discussing
Joseph, he says that we do not want to call Joseph a type (picture or pattern) of Christ, since the Bible is silent about such typology. "Nevertheless,
there are such remarkable parallels between Joseph and Christ that we
cannot neglect to be taught by them."[17] He then goes on to identify these
connections.[18]

Schaeffer's concern was to defend a Bible that is rational. The Bible
speaks propositionally, he often insisted. While he recognized that not
every statement in Scripture is a proposition, he staunchly defended the
clarity of Scripture. God speaks with "propositional communication,"
not requiring a leap of faith.[19] In an appendix to *He Is There and He Is Not*

---

[14] *CW*, 4:321.
[15] For example, in the manner of Geerhardus Vos, *Biblical Theology: Old and New Testaments* (Grand Rapids: Eerdmans, 1948).
[16] Indeed, in premillennialist fashion he taught that there were two portions to Old Testament prophecy,
one spiritual and the other national. We are still waiting for the second portion to be fulfilled (*CW*, 3:160).
[17] *CW*, 3:68.
[18] Here he follows the "literal-where-possible" method of dispensationalists, although he would have
objected to the comparison.
[19] *CW*, 1:120.

*Silent* he asks the question, "Is Propositional Revelation Nonsense?"[20] The answer is a resounding negative. The reason is that God the Creator is both personal and infinite, whereas we humans are personal but finite.[21] If God chooses to communicate, he can do so because of the link from his personality to ours. And because God cares about his human creatures, he communicates clearly, and thus propositionally. To withhold such communication would be unloving. Schaeffer cites a favorite example, where Jesus gave propositional revelation to Saul in the Hebrew language, using normal words and syntax.[22] The importance of this, as noted earlier, is that revelation is understandable, in human language. If God had not revealed himself verbally, then Saul would only have had some "first-order experience," and not a true revelation.

Having said this, however, Schaeffer adds that the Bible is a book for fallen creatures. The Bible gives us what we need to know in order to understand the central thrust, but it does not give all the details we could wish for. That would require an enormous library! Still, when it addresses science, the cosmos, and so on, it does speak truly. As he puts it: "Wherever it touches upon anything, it does so with true truth, but not with exhaustive truth. . . . Where it touches history, it speaks of what I call true truth—that is, propositional, objective truth."[23]

While he does not explore to any significant extent the genres and the literary structure of various books, Schaeffer nevertheless uses the Bible imaginatively. For example, he has a sermon on the theme "The Hand of God."[24] The metaphor of the hand is used to bring assurance to the people of God in six ways: (1) the hand of God creates; (2) the hand of God preserves; (3) the hand of God chastises; (4) the hand of God cares for his people; (5) the hand of God provides security; (6) the hand of God invites. In each case Schaeffer uses portions of Scripture that connect God's hands with these themes. The overall point is that God is personal and accessible. In another sermon he compares Elijah to Elisha.[25] Instead of using these two prophetic giants in a typical redemptive-historical manner, he makes

---

[20] *CW*, 1:345–49.
[21] Schaeffer received some criticism for this formulation. Cornelius Van Til was concerned that identifying personality as a common trait between God and human beings could give the impression of a univocal epistemology, whereas the Creator-creature distinction needs to be maintained at every level. Schaeffer's goal was to defend man's unique ability to receive rational revelation, rather than to construct an exhaustive ontology.
[22] *CW*, 1:347.
[23] *CW*, 2:52.
[24] *CW*, 3:15–26.
[25] *CW*, 3:99–106.

them examples. Elijah was constantly in the presence of great rulers, whereas Elisha's ministry was quieter. Thus, we should be just as happy to exercise a low-profile ministry and not seek the more rare dramatic life.

### Worldview Spirituality

What does the Bible teach? More (far more) but not less than the gospel story. Schaeffer was not an academic theologian. We will not find him exploring the finer points of the *ordo salutis* (the order of the various graces within our union with Christ: effectual calling, regeneration, faith, justification, adoption, sanctification, and glorification). Schaeffer was not interested in doing formal systematic theology. To be sure, he was doctrinally aware and stood within the contours of the Reformed faith. And yet he was always fresh. Most often, he set forth doctrines in a way that expressed apologetic and pastoral concerns. For example, in his talk-turned-article "Some Absolute Limits," he could have described the complex relationship between predestination and free will. But instead he talks of God as governed by neither chance nor determinism. He affirms that history has meaning and significance.[26]

So, where does the biblical worldview begin for Francis Schaeffer? First, God, the Holy Trinity, is preexistent. Fran often spoke of the way things were "before the beginning." He refers to places such as John 17:5, 24, which say that there was love, glory, and purposefulness before the world began. While history as such only began with the creation of the world, yet there was "sequence" in the life of the Holy Trinity.[27] Focusing on eternity in such a manner allowed Schaeffer to make a number of philosophical points. For him, God's eternity contradicts any idea of an impersonal beginning. Since God is both infinite and personal, pantheism (where the principle of god is impersonal) fails altogether. For another, it allows modern people to answer the question, where does love come from? Third, it clearly portrays Jesus Christ as an eternal person, and not merely an earthly one. Schaeffer insists that Christ "was already there before the creation and was active in creation."[28]

Second, the universe is God's creation. God made everything that exists, both visible and invisible. And he made it good. He made mankind

---

[26] CW, 4:167–71.
[27] CW, 2:9–14.
[28] CW, 2:13.

in his image. This is a critically important doctrine for Francis Schaeffer. He spent a good amount of time speaking and writing about the nobility and privilege of the human race. Though he very much believed in the corrupting power of sin, his doctrine of man made him a staunch defender of the right to life, over against many contemporary voices that were trying to undermine it. Today, people are asking, who am I? But the question cannot be answered within a closed system, that is, a universe not governed by the infinite-personal God. With the *imago Dei* we have the answer to "personality," and we have a reason for love. We also have a divine calling to have dominion over the earth.[29] Although he did not treat the *imago* systematically, it is clear from his statements about it that the image of God is constitutional more than functional. In the *Basic Bible Studies*, under Genesis 1:26 Schaeffer states that to be in God's image is glorious. The essence of the image is summed up in four principal attributes within man: his morality, rationality, creativity, and love.[30]

And then, third, there is the catastrophic event that changes all of history: the fall. The distinction between creation and the fall is fundamental to Schaeffer's theology, and he constantly railed against anyone who would confuse the two. Paul Tillich, for example, said that "man equals fallen man," and that if there was a fall, it was *upward*.[31] But Schaeffer believed that the fall into sin occurred in history. Its effects are all around us and are both intensive and extensive. Always the apologist, Schaeffer reminds us that the Bible is the most realistic book in the world, because it calls a spade a spade. Death is the result of the fall. And death means separation: first, between human beings and God; second, between parts of the self and other parts of the self (a sort of spiritual schizophrenia); third, between one human being and another; fourth, between mankind and the world (which man was meant to govern but which now swallows up humanity). Everything is now abnormal.[32] Humanity does not lose its *imago*, but struggles with all the tasks originally assigned.

Fourth, Jesus Christ is central to all of Schaeffer's theology. He is the Son of God. He became man through the incarnation. Perhaps unguardedly, Schaeffer says that in relation to God, ontologically, there is a chasm between all of creation and God; but as to "personality," God and man

---

[29] *CW*, 2:33–34.
[30] *CW*, 2:329.
[31] *CW*, 2:38.
[32] *CW*, 2:59–71.

are one.[33] I say unguardedly because we could get the impression from Schaeffer that the Creator-creature difference is not as great as it is according to Scripture. What Schaeffer is trying to do here is to make sure the image of God serves to keep a relationship between us and God viable. He may also be arguing for the mystical relationship between Christ and his church. He argues that Christ could not have become, say, an ant. But he could become a human being, since we are made after God's image. The same goes for communication between human beings. He strongly denounces any thought that our different backgrounds and cultures can succeed in preventing true communication between people.[34]

In classical fashion, Schaeffer says that Christ is prophet, priest, and king.[35] He was humiliated, then exalted.[36] He is the second Adam.[37] Jesus died for the sins of his people. This death was substitutionary, that is, Jesus died in the place of his people, taking their sins upon himself.[38] And Jesus was raised up from the dead.[39] Schaeffer spends a great deal of time defending the historicity of the resurrection. This was a major battlefield for his time (and still is, of course). The resurrection, he always insisted, occurred in "verifiable history," the same frame of reference that applies in scientific investigation.[40] Finally, Christ will return to the earth in personal and visible fashion. Commenting on the expression "the coming of the Son of Man" (Matt. 24:37) Schaeffer explains that the word "coming" is the word for *presence*. He adds, "There is coming a future time when Jesus will be present on earth—historically, space-time present in the same way as He was on earth when He spoke these words."[41] And the day is coming when creation will be restored, and our own bodies raised from the dead.[42]

Fifth, salvation comes to those who lift the empty hands of faith and receive Jesus Christ. Immediately upon turning to the Lord in faith, we are justified. "When I truly accept Christ as my Savior, the Bible says God declares me justified at once. God, as the Judge, judicially declares the guilt gone, upon the basis of the substitutionary work of Christ. . . . My

---

[33] CW, 1:102–3.
[34] CW, 2:104.
[35] CW, 3:338–44.
[36] CW, 2:344–46.
[37] CW, 2:74–76.
[38] CW, 2:74–77; 3:45.
[39] CW, 3:104–6.
[40] CW, 5:401.
[41] CW, 2:93.
[42] CW, 2:43.

sin has been punished, in Christ: in history, space and time, upon the cross."[43] Schaeffer is ever the apologist and also the pastor when discussing justification. "Nothing is left to be charged to our account," he asserts. There are no degrees in justification; you either are a Christian or you are not. If you are, then justification has occurred in the past, and the guilt is "gone forever."[44]

Sixth, it is a different matter for sanctification, which does come in degrees. Sanctification will be the subject of our subsequent discussions. For now, as we saw earlier, the point is that one cannot begin on the journey of sanctification without first being justified. Sanctification may be the more important portion of salvation, since it is ongoing, whereas justification is once and for all.[45] As in marriage, the wedding day has its place, a wonderful place, but it is just the beginning of a lifelong relationship, with its ups and downs.[46]

Seventh, and finally, there is glorification. Following in the way of Jesus's glorification, believers are glorified at death, and then at the resurrection.[47] The general resurrection occurs at the second advent of Jesus Christ. The resurrection to life, for believers, is followed by life in the new heavens and the new earth. For the lost, it is a resurrection unto death.[48] Throughout his writings, Schaeffer insists that this return to earth is visible and occurs in space and in time. He calls it a *brute fact*.[49] But he also insists that this fact is not just a promise or proposition, but a truth meant to give meaning to our present lives.[50]

---

[43] *CW*, 3:267.

[44] *CW*, 3:267–68.

[45] It is interesting to note that John Calvin, in the *Institutes*, discusses sanctification (3.6–10) before justification (3.11–16). While there is no doubt an apologetical reason for this, countering accusations of antinomianism made against Protestants, there is also a theological reason. More than simply receiving divine acquittal (justification), the Christian life (sanctification) is the goal of biblical religion.

[46] Schaeffer often used the analogy of marriage for the Christian life, which was not always appreciated by single folks. Similarly, for example, his teaching on the fatherhood of God might at first be difficult to hear for an abused child. These are analogies, and they are limited. Of course, every human relationship is inadequate by comparison to the divine model.

[47] Traditional Protestant theology most often speaks of glorification as occurring at the resurrection. See John Murray, *Redemption Accomplished and Applied* (Grand Rapids: Eerdmans, 1955), 174. However, it does also speak of the departed soul as having "entered into glory."

[48] As mentioned earlier, Schaeffer was a historic premillennialist, but he only rarely alluded to this eschatological scheme in his writings, although some have argued that his rise-and-fall historiography is connected with premillennialism, since it sees the coming of a great tribulation in the future. A lively debate has been engaged as to the possible connections between premillennial eschatology and declinism. If such a connection is there for Francis Schaeffer, we lack solid evidence to demonstrate it.

[49] Inasmuch as Schaeffer was not trained in formal philosophy, we may imagine that he was not acquainted with the distinction made by Elizabeth Anscombe (who likely coined the term) between brute facts and institutional facts. And he may have chosen not to acknowledge the attack on brute facts by his teacher Cornelius Van Til, who argued, along with Berkeley and against empiricism, that there are no uninterpreted facts (because of the ubiquity of God's revelation).

[50] *CW*, 4:175.

Francis Schaeffer strongly believed in the gospel message. But he placed it within the larger view of the world and of life that the Bible articulates. All in all, Francis Schaeffer was a Reformed eclectic. While he stood squarely in the Reformation tradition and presumably studied the Protestant classics in seminary, his views and expressions were shaped by many sources, including his own reflections and the things he learned in conversations. It is no surprise, then, that he set forth the great fundamentals in an established, orthodox manner, but yet with considerable creativity.

### Reality's Contours

At the heart of Francis Schaeffer's views on sanctification lies a theme that was indeed central to almost everything in his life and work, the theme of *reality*. This comes across over and over in *True Spirituality*. As mentioned above, focusing on reality is also a crucial part of the Schaeffers' journey. A quick look at the index for the complete works reveals nearly sixty references to "reality." Some of them refer to thorough treatments of the subject; others to passing allusions. But it is clear that Fran was consistently preoccupied with the matter of reality. We have seen that remedying the lack of reality in his life was what launched him into the work of L'Abri. What is meant in the uses of this particular concept?

1. In matters of philosophy and Christian apologetics, reality for Fran means the objective truth of the world and the Creator behind it. When trying to reason with unbelievers about the reliability of their morality, or their "mannishness," Schaeffer often referred to the "objective reality of the external world." The final reality is not chance, or even the Bible, but God himself.[51] For a method of apologetics, his preferred tactic was to square a person with reality. If someone persists in unbelief, then we may push him, gently but firmly, into the "logical conclusions of his presuppositions," which will have the effect of pulling him away from the real world, and thus showing him how dark it is away from reality.[52] Illustrations abound. Lovers on the left bank of the river Seine know something real about the universe.[53] Indeed, love is real because there is a real reason to keep the human race alive and not plunge humanity into death.[54]

---

[51] *CW*, 4:106.
[52] *CW*, 1:133, 140–42.
[53] *CW*, 1:24.
[54] *CW*, 1:79.

Further, the reason one can trust in the historic Christian position at all is that it is realistic about evil.[55] Without this realism there is no hope. The Christian view is neither optimistic nor nihilistic, but realistic.[56] And, as mentioned, theological realism also includes the reality of sin. Schaeffer often alluded to the Bible's brutal honesty about sin. Are we shocked by sin? We shouldn't be, since it is predicted over and over again in Scripture.[57] Nor are biblical concepts merely symbols, but they are real because based upon "the God who is there and who has spoken about himself."[58] Science can succeed because the same God who created the real world also made our minds to recognize it.[59]

2. Schaeffer loved to point to some of the hard facts of theology and earthly life as making sense only in the presence of God. A constant theme in Schaeffer's preaching and writing is the utter reality of the supernatural. We will have occasion to look at his views in some detail. But here it is worth noting that the unseen world is a very present, almost palpable, reality, contrary to what many of us experience.[60] In *True Spirituality* he devotes an entire chapter to "The Supernatural Universe," and in *Death in the City* he adds a remarkable text, "The Universe and Two Chairs," an appeal to live in light of the reality of the invisible world.[61] Non-Christians live in unbelief. Christians often live in "unfaith," that is, the functional denial of a fully supernatural world. From prayer to more ordinary activities such as eating a meal, nothing should be isolated from the "chair of faith." The very human activity of eating a meal is full of implications for the beauty of Christian living. About eating in our future, resurrection bodies, he says, "Among the many things which are marvelous about this is the very reality of it—the solidness of it."[62] Many of us love the picture in the Gospels of the disciples marveling at the sight of the resurrected Jesus as he says, in effect, "Got anything to eat?" (Luke 24:41).

3. While Schaeffer taught that we should expect progress in the Christian life, he strongly warned against perfectionism. Only the reality

---

[55] *CW*, 1:45.
[56] *CW*, 1:46.
[57] *CW*, 3:29, 87.
[58] *CW*, 1:61.
[59] *CW*, 1:335.
[60] *CW*, 2:156; 3:246.
[61] *True Spirituality* (Wheaton, IL: Tyndale, 1972), chap. 5; *Death in the City* (Downers Grove, IL: InterVarsity, 1969; reissued, Wheaton, IL: Crossway, 2002), chap. 9.
[62] *CW*, 2:155.

of Christ's accomplishment can keep us where we need to be. Though God's perfection is the standard, there can be no perfection*ism* this side of the resurrection.[63] He often pointed out that marriage problems arise when one of the spouses expects "perfection or nothing," which would inevitably lead to getting "nothing." This too is related to *reality*. As we experience the Christian life in general, our conscience may be quieted when we have a better grasp of the present reality of the finished work of Christ.

> All of us battle with the problem of reality. . . . If I lay hold upon the blood of Christ in faith, reality rests here—not in trying to live as though the Bible teaches perfectionism. . . . But there is a reality here: the reality of sins forgiven. . . . Reality is not meant to be only creedal, though creeds are important. Reality is to be experienced on the basis of a restored relationship with God through the finished work of the Lord Jesus Christ on the cross.[64]

4. Finally, if Christians are to meet the challenges of the day, they must acknowledge "two contents and two realities."[65] This is Schaeffer's creative way of stressing the need for solid doctrine along with solid practice. The first "content" is sound doctrine. The second is honest answers to honest questions. The first "reality" is true spirituality, and the second is "the beauty of human relationships." Metaphysically, of course, there is only one, final reality.[66] But to stress the utter importance of personal sanctification as well as loving human relations, Fran dubs them *realities*.

Schaeffer's thinking had a number of affinities with the philosophy of realism, as I have mentioned. However, it would be a mistake to label him a pure philosophical realist, or even a Scottish Common Sense realist. His use of the term *reality*, particularly when referring to the Christian life, is informal. He means to say that God is real; the presence of God can really be known in our experience. There is an objective basis for human experience. Realism for him is an antidote not for idealism, as it might be in philosophical debates, but for spiritual dryness. Schaeffer has been dubbed a realist in the sense of the Old Princeton apologetics of Archibald

---

[63] *CW*, 4:177; 3:288.
[64] *CW*, 3:297–98.
[65] *CW*, 3:407–22.
[66] *CW*, 4:289.

Alexander, Charles Hodge, and B. B. Warfield. However, it is not clear that Schaeffer would have consciously espoused their views. Besides, the philosophical label of realism is likely misapplied to the Old Princeton, as Paul Helseth argues in a recent book.[67]

In any case, it would be hard to overstate the critical importance of reality for Schaeffer's approach to the Christian life. He was deeply concerned to experience the presence of God and then show others the way to live in that same reality.

---

[67] Paul K. Helseth, *"Right Reason" and the Princeton Mind: An Unorthodox Proposal* (Phillipsburg, NJ: P&R, 2010).

# CHAPTER 5

# FREEDOM IN THE CHRISTIAN LIFE

*Therefore when I seek to obey God's commandments, I am not work-*
*ing against myself, but for myself. I am acting in accordance with my*
*nature as the image of God. As I do what is right I establish my true*
*identity: I free myself!*

RANALD MACAULAY AND
JERRAM BARRS

### Freedom Now

The main purpose of this chapter is to take a close look at the first portion
of the sermon series that became the book *True Spirituality*. We are fortu-
nate indeed that while we may and must look throughout the oeuvre of
Francis Schaeffer for themes relating to the Christian life, we do have such
a principal text to work with, the fruit of years of work, in which his major
reflections are delivered systematically. Accordingly, we find here in *True*
*Spirituality* that while *reality* is the central concern in matters pertaining to
the Christian life for Schaeffer, one of the most concrete manifestations of
the real is *freedom*. The two large sections of the series are titled "Freedom
Now from the Bonds of Sin" and "Freedom Now from the Results of Sin."
But freedom and reality are about the same kinds of issues, since to have
freedom is to make the gospel real. Throughout each section within these
two larger categories one finds teaching about applying the principles of

the gospel to our present lives. At the risk of being a bit pedantic, let us explore this series, not exhaustively, but respecting its main emphases in relation to the reality of freedom. The chapter headings are as follows:

| | |
|---|---|
| **Section I** | **Freedom Now from the Bonds of Sin** |
| Chapter 1 | The Law and the Law of Love |
| Chapter 2 | The Centrality of Death |
| Chapter 3 | Through Death to Resurrection |
| Chapter 4 | In the Spirit's Power |
| Chapter 5 | The Supernatural Universe |
| Chapter 6 | Salvation: Past-Future-Present |
| Chapter 7 | The Fruitful Bride |
| | |
| **Section II** | **Freedom Now from the Results of the Bonds of Sin** |
| Chapter 8 | Freedom from Conscience |
| Chapter 9 | Freedom in the Thought-life |
| Chapter 10 | Substantial Healing of Psychological Problems |
| Chapter 11 | Substantial Healing of the Total Person |
| Chapter 12 | Substantial Healing in Personal Relationships |
| Chapter 13 | Substantial Healing in the Church |

Appendix: The Dust of Life

The logic of this organization is simple, although the subjects of each chapter are not without overlap. Generally, the first major section is foundational. In it Schaeffer explains the biblical and theological underpinnings for the Christian life. The second major section applies these principles to various issues, such as conscience, personal relations, and the like. Schaeffer is quite insistent that this order cannot be reversed. Unless the foundations are established as "objectively true," then we have a psychological trick and a "cruel illusion," rather than the Christian life. Once again, as he puts it at the beginning of each major section, Fran establishes the critical principle that the gospel must be embraced before there can be any practice of the Christian life.[1]

This said, let us now walk through the major teachings in this remarkable series.

---

[1] CW, 3:199–201, 287–88.

## Two Tests

The first section, then, is titled, "Freedom Now from the Bonds of Sin." After certain preliminaries, which stress the necessity of being a Christian through the new birth, chapter 1 addresses the question, "What shall I do next?" The chapter introduces the matter of the human heart. Schaeffer remarks that in many cases new Christians are given a list of dos and don'ts. Although such lists may have had good reasons in their contexts, the Christian life is far more than a series of taboos.[2] But the answer for such lists is not antinomianism, the belief that we are free in Christ to live any way we like. "We do not come to true spirituality or the true Christian life merely by keeping a list, but neither do we come to it merely by rejecting the list and then shrugging our shoulders and living a looser life."[3] Given Schaeffer's background in the separated churches and his convictions about the Christian liberties, and then his reaction to some of the harshness of this approach, his twofold emphasis makes sense. Rules can lead to externalism. But some rules are needed for a godly Christian life. Indeed, the Ten Commandments are no ordinary list. They represent the law of love.

However, the fundamental issue is not a matter of lists, even at the high level of the law of love. Rather, the Christian life needs to be considered an *inward*, rather than an outward, reality. Although we should not call him a mystic, at least in the classical sense, Schaeffer constantly will point us to conscience, motive, a living faith, and matters of the heart. Here Schaeffer adeptly points out that the climax of the Ten Commandments is the law against coveting. Coveting is the negative way of expressing the positive commands. "Love is internal, not external," he argues, although both love and coveting will have external manifestations. When coming to this inward aspect of the law of love, we can say it is the voice of the Holy Spirit that prompts us.[4]

Schaeffer suggests two tests to help us evaluate whether we are coveting. The first test relates to God: do I know *contentment*? If I love God enough to be contented, then I am being properly spiritual. The opposite of contentment, he says, is *revolt*, which is the essence of sin. He presents a number of biblical proofs for this contention, particularly Romans 8:28,

[2] *CW*, 3:201.
[3] *CW*, 3:202.
[4] *CW*, 3:204.

which he maintains is not to candy-coat the evils of the world, but to assure us that even in the midst of terrible suffering, God will bring about the good. In a fallen, abnormal world, I can still believe that the universe is personal, and that God has the right to use me in the spiritual battle.[5]

The second test relates to our neighbor: do I love my neighbor enough not to envy? A number of manifestations of envy are cited. Do I take secret pleasure at my neighbor's misfortune? Schaeffer insists that we are all susceptible to this sin. Even in my quest for more reality I can fall into this perversion.[6] And if we are honest, we will realize that secret envy soon spills over into external life, so we can end up hating our neighbor and slandering him. Again Schaeffer adduces a number of biblical warrants for this test: 1 Corinthians 13, of course, but also Galatians 2:20 and Romans 6.

Finally, though, important as the negatives of revolt or envy may be, they are not the end of the story. The end must be positive: I am to be in communion with God in this present moment of history.[7]

### Death and Resurrection

After addressing these introductory issues, moving from externals to matters of the heart he looks at the most basic considerations of true spirituality: death and resurrection in Christ. In a way, dying and finding new life in and through Jesus Christ are the very center, the fundamental dynamic of the spiritual life for Francis Schaeffer.

In the spirit of the realism with which we have been acquainted, Fran underscores the hard fact of death.[8] Death is a very serious matter for him. Here, following passages such as Romans 6:4–6 and Galatians 2:20, he asserts two truths. We have died, and we must die daily. Saying no is a central dynamic of the Christian life. Yet its ultimate purpose is positive.

> Again we must say this is not just something to be taken romantically,
> to stir up some sort of an emotion within ourselves. It is a very strong
> negative word. We are to be willing to say "no" to ourselves, we are to be

---

[5] *CW*, 3:208. Interestingly, John Calvin has very similar thoughts about contentment. See the *Institutes*, 2.8.46.

[6] *CW*, 3:209.

[7] *CW*, 3:212.

[8] It has not escaped notice that the word *death* characterizes a good number of Francis Schaeffer's titles. We can think of *Death in the City* (1969), *Pollution and the Death of Man* (1970), but also of the numerous headings throughout his writings. His closest friend and colleague, Hans Rookmaaker, wrote a landmark study on the history of art called *Modern Art and the Death of a Culture* (1970).

willing to say "no" to things in order that the command to love God and men may have real meaning.[9]

So, while saying no is uncomfortable and goes against the grain of a permissive culture, it is the only way forward. Schaeffer makes quite an extended point about the fact that at the mount of transfiguration (Luke 9:27–36), where the disciples saw a prefiguring of Christ in his glory, the topic of conversation between Jesus, Moses, and Elijah was death. "You notice that they *kept speaking* of Christ's coming death."[10] The center of the Christian message is not Jesus's life or his miracles, but his death. The Ten Commandments themselves are largely negative. Despite the pain of denying our natural tendencies, it is the right way forward: "True spirituality does not stop at the negative, but without the negative—in comprehension and practice—we are not ready to go on."

From death we move to resurrection. Schaeffer begins with a splendid illustration from music. Now it is time for trumpets, he tells us. Jesus was rejected, slain, and then . . . he was raised! Again, using biblical passages such as the account of the transfiguration (a story he truly loves), and various accounts of Jesus's postresurrection appearances, he stresses the concrete, historical reality of the raised Savior. Again, he discusses the appearance of Jesus to Saul on the Damascus Road, and the heavenly vision of John on the Isle of Patmos.[11] These are so many proofs of the finished work of Christ, which now translate into reality for the believer. Thus, when we receive Christ, God looks upon us as dead and raised.[12] Because of this, we should live today as though we were dead to sin and alive to God.[13] Our lives are based not upon resignation or upon the effacement of the self, but upon an active yielding of our self, and a tending toward becoming "the creature glorified."[14]

Chapter 4 expands on this theme with an extended consideration of the present reality of the resurrection. The stress in this section is on the linkage between Christ and us through the Holy Spirit. Again, Schaeffer studies the transfiguration in light of several places in Scripture that tell of the resurrection of believers. Christians may experience a *true mysticism*,

[9] *CW*, 3:216.
[10] *CW*, 3:219–23.
[11] *CW*, 3:227–33.
[12] *CW*, 3:235.
[13] *CW*, 3:236–40.
[14] *CW*, 3:240.

he argues, not one of passivity, but an "active passivity."[15] Schaeffer spends some time on the story of Mary, who was told she would carry the Christ child. She could have either refused this privilege or tried to achieve it in her own strength. But instead, she said, "Behold, I am the servant of the Lord; let it be to me according to your word" (Luke 1:38). From this Schaeffer derives his idea of active passivity: "Consciously the power must not be of myself. It is the power of the crucified, risen, and glorified Christ, through the agency of the Holy Spirit, by faith."[16]

Although Schaeffer does not explicate the doctrine of sanctification with systematic-theological precision, his account strongly resembles the Reformed emphasis on *becoming who you are*. Often cast as "deriving the imperative from the indicative," the idea is that as Christians we are new creations. We *have* died to sin, and *do* sit in the heavenly places (see 2 Cor. 5:17; Col. 2:20; 3:1). For this reason we *ought* to live as though these realities are true. John Murray has coined the term "definitive sanctification" to explain that the Christian has already made a radical breach with sin and is already raised with Christ. This once-for-all grace is renovative and should not be confused with justification, which is forensic.[17] But being definitive, it gives us the dynamic for sanctification.[18]

Chapter 5 again visits the theme of reality. Titled "The Supernatural Universe," it takes up Schaeffer's constant preoccupation with the presence of the invisible world. For a more thorough discussion of this subject, one could look at the essay "The Universe and Two Chairs," which features as chapter 9 in *Death in the City*.[19] The essay explores the reality of the unseen world using the illustration of two people in a dark room with a closed door. The room represents the universe that God has made. But the person on the one chair cannot acknowledge anything more than a material world. The person on the other chair recognizes the reality of the unseen world.[20] The essay goes on to chide many Christians for sitting, in effect, on the chair of "unfaith," where functionally they might as well be living in a purely material world. So, here in chapter 5 of *True*

---

[15] CW, 3:263.

[16] CW, 3:253.

[17] John Murray, "Definitive Sanctification," in *The Collected Works of John Murray*, vol. 2, *Select Lectures in Systematic Theology* (Edinburgh: Banner of Truth, 1977), 277–84.

[18] See, for example, Douglas Moo, *The Epistle to the Romans* (Grand Rapids: Eerdmans, 1996), 391; and John Murray, *Principles of Conduct* (Grand Rapids: Eerdmans, 1974), 202–28.

[19] CW, 4:287–99.

[20] In this essay, though not elsewhere, Schaeffer suggests that even the term *supernatural* is not helpful, since the unseen world is just as natural, just as real, as the seen world.

*Spirituality*, Schaeffer reinforces the view that the Christian life is lived in light of the Bible's emphasis on the supernatural world. An idea that might be strange—for example, that Christ is the Bridegroom bearing fruit through us—becomes understandable if our world is truly supernatural. (He will pick up on this theme in chap. 7.) Schaeffer puts the matter of taking the supernatural seriously in the strongest terms: today the church has allowed the ceiling of the naturalistic to come down upon us, mixing the metaphor, "by injection or connotation."[21]

### Active Passivity

The burden of chapter 6 is to argue that while Christ's work of redemption is finished, and while we look forward to the day of our full redemption in the new heavens and new earth, yet there is tremendous work to be done here and now. The epoch between the cross and the second coming should not be seen as a parenthesis. Those familiar with the L'Abri story will recognize many of the emphases that were integral to the founding of this extraordinary work. Fran says that it is vain to preach the gospel without waiting on the Holy Spirit.[22] We might recall the day Fran asked Edith whether it would make any difference to their lives if all of the teaching on the Holy Spirit and prayer were literally removed from the Bible. In the present chapter he forcefully urges Christians to demonstrate the existence of God "at our point of history." He insists that we be a such demonstration not in the past or the future (except through our legacy), but in the present.[23] He also puts the matter theologically, stating that salvation begins with justification, but is far broader than our once-for-all acquittal.

Finally in part 1, a chapter on "The Fruitful Bride" more fully describes a theme that appears in other places in Schaeffer's writings.[24] Fruit bearing is also connected with Jesus's teaching about the vine and the branches, recorded in John 15. Schaeffer builds on these analogies to make his point that there should be palpable evidence for our primary relationship with the triune God. We can produce good fruit or bad fruit. In a manner not unlike some of the medieval mystics, he talks of Christ as "my lover," and

---

[21] *CW*, 3:263.
[22] *CW*, 3:266.
[23] *CW*, 3:266–67.
[24] See, for example, *The Church at the End of the Twentieth Century*, in *CW*, 4:47; *The Church Before the Watching World*, in *CW*, 4:133–49.

of the possibility of being faithful or unfaithful to him.[25] Unfaithfulness is spiritual adultery, which is what sin is, and it can give birth to a child from the wrong husband.[26] Here he further reinforces the key themes from his earlier words. Our practice should be moment by moment, one incident at a time, as the existentialists have properly recognized. He returns to the idea of "active passivity," which Mary exhibited. He speaks against any sort of mechanical approach to true spirituality.[27] Instead, there is to be personal communion.

It might be possible to misunderstand fruit bearing, moment-by-moment practice, and "active passivity," and to bring undue pressure upon oneself to cultivate some sort of Christian existentialism. I personally experienced such a weight when I first heard this material. As a new Christian I found myself under pressure to try and practice the presence of God at every moment. I remember walking up the street at Harvard, trying to force my brain into an almost electronic kind of plug-in to God. It was not very healthy.

When I understood things a bit better, I realized that Schaeffer was pleading for us to be conscious of our comportment. That was all right, but still not quite feasible for me. It helped me to go on and read the more classical Reformed theologians and discover the quiet confidence I could have because Jesus Christ had finished his work, and thus I need not, in a sense, try to finish it for him! I was also greatly helped by John Murray's teaching on "definitive sanctification," mentioned above. Murray also helped me to have a better grasp on the relation of redemption to the original creation. Because there is a continuity between the creation—with its ordinances, such as work, rest, worship, procreation—and the post-fallen world that is being redeemed, it began to dawn on me that I was not expected to enter into a pressured degree of self-consciousness about my spirituality, as though everything started from scratch. Certainly, I should be responsible and "work out [my] salvation with fear and trembling," as the apostle enjoins (Phil. 2:12). But as he goes on to say, "it is God who works in [me], both to will and to work" (v. 13).

Although Schaeffer surely believed in the permanent value of the creation ordinances (labor, worship, marriage and family, etc.), I do not

---

[25] Bernard de Clairvaux (1090–1153), for example, interpreted the Song of Songs in a series of sermons describing the soul as the bride and Christ as the bridegroom, going so far as to consider the mystical union as nuptials.
[26] CW, 3:276.
[27] CW, 3:280–82.

remember much discussion of the *cultural mandate* at L'Abri, nor of the connection between the *imago* and the command to fill the earth and subdue it (Gen. 1:26–30; Ps. 8:5–8; Jer. 29:4–7; Heb. 2:5–9, etc.).[28] It could be that this is simply a matter of terminology. He expressed to Ranald Macaulay and Jerram Barrs that their book *Being Human* fully reflects what he had been trying to say. That book is full of insights into cultural engagement.[29] While Fran certainly was committed to an important place for culture and the arts in the Christian life, and the emphases brought into the theological and philosophical worlds by Abraham Kuyper on such things as "sphere sovereignty" were lurking in the background, he rarely alluded in so many words to Kuyper and the neo-Calvinist movement. Yet he was clearly at home with many of their emphases. His closest friend, Hans Rookmaaker, did so far more often. Since Rookmaaker worked at the Dutch L'Abri, one could say that his teaching fully qualifies as L'Abri teaching. And, furthermore, it should be said that Schaeffer deeply admired the way Calvinism had influenced Dutch culture in the post-Reformation years.[30]

Schaeffer does say, here in "The Fruitful Bride" and elsewhere, that the Christian life is a *restoration* to what I am meant to be; as a Christian I become who I was intended to be as God's image bearer.[31] He states that the only difference between our relationship with the Lord now (in the era of redemption) and in the original order of creation ("that which man's [relationship] would have been had he not sinned") is that we are now under the covenant of grace, rather than the covenant of works. At present our relationship rests on the basis of Christ's finished mediatorial work, and that is the only difference.[32]

Such a point of view is very much rooted in the Reformed heritage. It is the opposite of Platonism. Just as there is continuity between our present sanctification and the original pre-fallen creation, so there is some measure of continuity between our present world and the world to come. Again, Schaeffer does not discuss the details in technical theological terms. Of course, even Reformed theologians vary in their interpretations

---

[28] Today, I am inclined to call this the "civilizational mandate" for various reasons.
[29] Jerram Barrs and Ranald Macaulay, *Being Human: The Nature of Spiritual Experience* (Downers Grove, IL: InterVarsity, 1998).
[30] Schaeffer takes a bow before Kuyper's notion of sphere sovereignty in *Pollution and the Death of Man*, which we will look at in chap. 8 (*CW*, 5:35). Here and there he does allude to the cultural mandate, though under different names. One is the term *dominion*. See *Genesis in Space and Time* (*CW*, 2:35).
[31] *CW*, 3:283.
[32] *CW*, 3:283.

of the biblical data. Thus, at one end of the spectrum, the new heavens and new earth are viewed as a restoration to the original, Edenic state, except that there is no temptation or capacity to fall again. At the other end of the spectrum, the present life is believed to move deliberately toward a renewed earth, one in which today's culture and technology and city-building are validated in the eschaton. Geerhardus Vos argues that the purpose of the test in Eden, whereby God forbade our first parents to take of the fruit of the tree of the knowledge of good and evil, was to enable mankind to grow and mature. Had Adam and Eve resisted the serpent's suggestion, they would have led humanity from the sinless life in the garden to eternal life, a life of confirmed, consummate bliss. The tree of life represents the future of humanity.[33]

Where Francis Schaeffer stood on some of these details is not clear. After studying at seminary, in typical fashion I would ask him some of these questions. His reflections were always fascinating, but rarely conversant with the more academic literature. As far as I could discover, he did not reflect upon the tree of life as an eschatological sign or upon what would have happened had Adam and Eve passed the probation. For Schaeffer, this test was a simple one to measure their allegiance to God and to demonstrate that they had free will.[34] This point cannot be stressed too much. Using the "free-will defense," Schaeffer always insisted that what may have looked like gross unfairness—the taking of one fruit leading to such unspeakable wreckage—was to him proof of human significance. So much responsibility was built into God's image bearers that our apparently minor decisions can affect eternity.

When our first parents failed, God intervened graciously to establish the covenant of grace. Salvation means a present reality, and then going to heaven. While he was reluctant to go into detail, Fran did affirm that heaven is more than a return to square one. Heaven is "non-static," he often remarked, a place where we will recognize loved ones, a place where learning and work will go on forever, but without the drudgery or anxiety we experience at the present time. At the end of his booklet *Art and the Bible*

---

[33] Geerhardus Vos, *Biblical Theology: Old and New Testaments* (Grand Rapids: Eerdmans, 1948), 37–51.

[34] The question of free agency is fraught with peril. Henri Blocher warns against using the free-will argument to explain the problem of evil because it implies that God placed the possibility of a fault into his creation (*Evil and the Cross: An Analytical Look at the Problem of Pain* [Downers Grove, IL: InterVarsity, 1994], 14). So concerned is he not to justify or excuse evil that he denies the typically Reformed idea of the probation. John Calvin reluctantly uses the expression *free will*, since the Fathers used it, but his concern is that it not translate into merit of any kind (*Institutes*, 2.2.5). Schaeffer did use it, principally because of his defense of human significance, over against any kind of determinism.

he suggests that Swiss painter Paul Robert had it right when on a mural in Neuchâtel he showed a lovely stairway leading to heaven, with beautiful people ascending and carrying symbols of several art forms, including architecture and music. They are ascending, and Christ is descending to accept these treasures. Paul Robert "also knew that if these things are to be carried up to the praise of God and the Lordship of Christ at the second coming, then we should be offering them to God now. . . . The reality of the future has meaning for the present!"[35]

---

[35] *CW*, 2:391.

# CHAPTER 6

# APPLICATIONS

*When conscience did speak, you said, "Lay down, sir, be quiet!" When God's word came home sharp to you, you tried to blunt its edge—you did not want to feel it. Now, ought it not to be some comfort that you have had such a gracious change wrought in you, that you are now longing for the very feeling which at one time you could not endure? Surely, man, the Lord must have begun a good work in you, for you would not have such wishes and desires as these unless he had put his hand to the plough, and had begun to plough the barren, dry, hard soil of your heart.*

CHARLES SPURGEON

### A Clear Conscience

In the next major section of *True Spirituality* Schaeffer moves from the more foundational considerations of freedom from the bonds of sin to some wider, more practical considerations, suggesting various applications flowing from the principles. Accordingly, the title of this second part is "Freedom Now from the Results of the Bonds of Sin." Once again, he begins by insisting that applications make no sense, indeed they are cruel, unless they are based squarely on first things. Here, he mentions three, a variant on his other lists: (1) the objective reality of the supernatural universe, (2) the existence of the personal-infinite God with men in his image, (3) and man's true moral guilt.

He addresses the issue of death as separation. The fall resulted in several types of separation: from God, from each other, from nature, and from ourselves. Schaeffer comments on each of these separations. His particular focus in these chapters is on the way the fall has affected ourselves (chaps. 8–11) and our relationships (chaps. 12–13).

First, he looks at various ways to address separation from ourselves, or what we might call psychological issues. He looks at freedom of the conscience in chapter 8. Here, he signals two preliminaries—two things to avoid—crucial to his later discussion. The first is perfectionism. We encountered this same concern earlier, in the treatment of reality. Here, the question of perfectionism serves as an entry point into the subject of conscience. While Schaeffer would show some sympathies with John Wesley's views, here he warns against Wesleyan perfectionism. He states that the earlier Wesley taught that perfection in the life of a believer is possible from a certain point on. Discovering that such a notion is unrealistic, however, Wesley later modified his views. Schaeffer could never approve of any form of perfectionism, yet he nevertheless thought Wesley was seeking something right: aspiring to experiencing the reality of the present value of Christ's finished work.[1]

In fact, John Wesley's views on perfectionism are somewhat complex. Even before the famous Aldersgate Street experience of 1738, where he felt his heart to have been warmed by the gospel, Wesley believed that the Christian could achieve a state of perfection. Afterward, he refined his idea by claiming that the Christian could have a *heart* in which the love for God and neighbor may be achieved instantaneously in the present life. This is probably the distinction Schaeffer is referring to, although reading Wesley on the subject of perfection is fairly confusing. At any rate, Wesley did teach that one could attain a state of perfection by claiming God's promises expectantly and with empty hands. This is not sinless perfection, which he never taught. Even when one arrives at perfection, there is still progress to be made, and errors to be overcome.[2] While Wesley's position is more nuanced than is sometimes thought, the net result is "entire sanctification," a state wherein the Holy Spirit in a moment roots out every motive from the believer's heart except love.

No doubt it is this "in a moment" aspect that Schaeffer is thinking about. This work is wrought objectively by the Spirit, but it is felt subjec-

---

[1] *CW*, 3:288, 295.
[2] See Albert Outler, ed., *John Wesley* (New York: Oxford University Press, 1964), 257ff.

tively by the assurance that we are in a heightened state of prayer, praise, and freedom from the bonds of sin.[3] Of course, as Schaeffer rightly saw, Wesley's view stands in tension with both the Bible's realistic view of the pervasiveness of sin and the revelation of God's demands for perfect holiness, a state we may achieve only in the new heavens and the new earth.

Schaeffer's view of a deepening experience, or set of experiences, which can be sought in the Christian life, is profoundly unperfectionist. Complete victory in a moment is bound to get us "caught in a swamp" where we cannot even decide what it is we are trying to attain. The notion of "freedom from known sin," which is often how this experience is referred to, is absolutely impossible, since our natures are very deep. Indeed the best of us is "separated from himself."[4] We are so deeply fallen that only Christ can plumb the depths of our beings and unleash his sanctifying power.

A second preliminary is Schaeffer's insistence that we not think lightly or abstractly of sin in our lives. One way to do this is to count on Christ's victory for our passage into heaven, but then be blind to the need for victory in the present battles of this life.[5] Practical victory now is available through Christ, who was tempted but never sinned.

The body of the chapter is a discussion of the sordid reality of sin, and then the great power of Christ over that sin, which leads to freedom from the bondage of conscience. Sin can enter a number of ways. Christians can grow cold and can allow sin to creep in, even to the point where there appears to be no difference between them and unbelievers. But there is a way back, and that is the very same way we came into faith in the first place: the blood of Christ.[6] God may have to chastise us to get our attention, as a father does with his children (Heb. 12:5–11). When this happens, Schaeffer enjoins us to name the sin, and to go through our own garden of Gethsemane experience, where we say to God, "Not my will, but yours, be done." He repeats previous considerations, such as the multilevel complexity of the human psyche, the need to lift the empty hands of faith, and the need for "active passivity."

Schaeffer states that the Reformation heritage is weak on recognizing the present reality, or the conscious side of the Christian life. Here he

---

[3] One of the most illuminating treatments of Wesleyan perfectionism from a Reformed point of view is J. I. Packer, *Keep in Step with the Spirit: Finding Fullness in Our Walk with God*, rev. ed. (Grand Rapids: Baker, 2005), 110–19.
[4] *CW*, 3:289.
[5] *CW*, 3:290.
[6] *CW*, 3:292.

praises Wesley for having known the present reality of Christ's work, even though his theology was not right. The answer for coldness is not a "second blessing," but the reality of Christ's work in the present life.[7]

It is hard to know what to say here. We saw as we looked at Fran and Edith's life that they had encountered some Reformed folks whom they deemed guilty of "cold orthodoxy." There certainly exists a type who claims to be Reformed and yet lacks the warmth and piety that Reformed theology so strongly commends. We have all met such folks. They are grim indeed. But is it fair to paint with such a large brush? When you read John Calvin's works or John Owen's treatises or Charles Spurgeon's sermons, let alone the more recent Reformed theologians, such as Herman Bavinck or John Murray, you find a marvelous marriage of high orthodoxy and warm piety. Indeed, I have come to think that the expression "cold orthodoxy" is an oxymoron, though of course I know what is meant.

At any rate, sin does invade us, and yet we can know the reality of a clear conscience now. Schaeffer recounts how he has struggled over the years with his own conscience. After a sin is dealt with, on the basis of Christ's finished work, the conscience can still bother us. He pictures his conscience as a big black dog that leaps up and covers him with mud. He has to turn toward it and say, in effect, "Down! Be still!"[8] Once cleansed, I am clean, and it is time to move back into the battle, freed from the false tyranny of conscience. There is no double jeopardy!

### Properly Inward

Still discussing spirituality in relation to our separation from ourselves, or psychological issues, Schaeffer then tackles the internal world of thought in chapter 9. Actually, this chapter does some basic apologetics. Schaeffer goes through Romans 1, and he explicates how general revelation affects our thought world. Similar material can be found in other places in his writing, particularly *Death in the City*. The reason this appears in a book on spirituality is that Schaeffer is convinced that sin and folly have affected our souls. Following Romans 1, he shows how God makes himself known in both the external world and the internal world of thought, but humanity rejects that knowledge. Schaeffer stresses that human error is not only

---

[7] *CW*, 3:295.
[8] Consciously or not, Schaeffer is using an image from Winston Churchill's biographer. See Lord Moran, *Churchill: The Struggle for Survival* (London: Constable, 1966), 179, 195, 794.

in regard to the form, but also, and more especially, in regard to the content of what God clearly reveals.

Perhaps in keeping with the tradition that says "ideas have consequences," Schaeffer places the thought world at the center of the Christian life.[9] Here and throughout his writings, he stresses the priority of the mind. Even moral battles are first fought not in the external world, but in the mind.[10] Schaeffer states this very strongly. At times it seems an overreach. For example, he tries to prove the primacy of the thought world with the passage where Jesus says that the mouth speaks out of the abundance of the heart (Matt. 12:34). But surely the biblical idea of the heart is richer than the mind and its thoughts (although it includes the mind). He cites the anthropologist Loren Eiseley to support his view. Eiseley once said that at some point in evolution "man has entered his own head, and he has been adapting ever since to what he finds there."[11] Jerram Barrs reminds me that Schaeffer was more nuanced than many may think. While he did focus on the mind, he often insisted that the truth is more than merely rational. Because of his concern that modern people were using the irrational as something to be emulated, he could sound as though he were touting the purely rational. But in fact he was very close to the biblical norm of the human heart, with its concomitant emphasis on creativity and beauty.[12]

Schaeffer also says that not only does the mind cause what happens externally, but also the mind itself can be sinful. Here, we find him reflecting the Reformed idea of the noetic effects of sin. And he equates the thought world with free will. Again, in the Reformed tradition, "free will," or free agency, does not defend human autonomy, but describes human responsibility. Thus, Reformed theology wants fully to recognize the ethical nature of the thought process. Perhaps in a way that could lead some of his followers to downplay the sovereignty of God, Schaeffer says that because of this anthropology, "there is a true first cause." As he puts it in several places, Adam was unprogrammed. The introduction of evil into the world has its origin here, in the decision of the mind.[13] Using the free-will argument, Schaeffer affirms that love requires a choice, and if you can

[9] *CW*, 3:302. We do not know whether he read Richard Weaver's book *Ideas Have Consequences* (Chicago: University of Chicago Press, 1948). The book was enormously influential and inspired conservatives in the postwar period to fight against relativism and "nominalism." Some of Weaver's historiography is remarkably similar to Schaeffer's.
[10] *CW*, 3:302.
[11] *CW*, 3:304.
[12] Jerram Barrs, e-mail message to author, October 30, 2011.
[13] *CW*, 3:305.

choose to say yes, you have to be able to choose to say no. But that choice comes from the mind. The process parallels God himself, since he first thought, then spoke, following which the world came into being.[14]

If Schaeffer is aware of the considerable literature evaluating the free-will argument, he does not interact with it. His concern is to preserve a certain balance. He denies pantheism, where the human creature is but an extension of divine essence. But he also denies the pure autonomy of the human choice maker, not so much because God has predestined all things (although Fran certainly believes that) but because God thought the whole thing up first. Fran illustrates this with the Sistine Chapel in Rome, where Michelangelo portrays the creation of man. Adam has just been made by the Ancient of Days, whose one arm is still stretched out. However, their fingers do not touch, showing forth the Creator-creature distinction. At the same time, nestled under God's other arm is a beautiful woman, presumably Eve, as yet uncreated. She is in the mind of God.

Again, Schaeffer does not go into any great detail in considering the rather thorny matter of God's full sovereignty in relation to the appearance of evil in the created world. It is clear from Scripture, as he affirms, that God's council precedes the creation of the world and every event in history (Acts 2:23; Rom. 8:29–30; 1 Pet. 1:2). He decrees whatsoever comes to pass. But does Schaeffer stop at the idea that God is simply *thinking* about what shall come to pass? Foreordination certainly qualifies as an idea of the future, but it is also an ordaining, a plan that will be executed (Eph. 1:11).

There is considerable mystery about how God could so ordain everything that comes to pass, yet without being accountable for evil. One traditional way of putting it is that while he freely ordains whatsoever comes to pass, yet he neither is the "author" of evil nor violates secondary causes (such as human decision), but rather sustains them.[15] Schaeffer was surely comfortable with this statement, since it was a part of his own confessional standard. But the question I am raising here is whether having an idea in the mind first, then bringing about its realization, is quite an adequate statement of the issue. It seems to me that personality, whether human or divine, involves more than simply thinking. Does not God's council and his ordaining of all things mean more (though not less) than having an idea and then making good on it?

---

[14] *CW*, 3:306.
[15] Westminster Confession of Faith 3.1.

Schaeffer is not particularly precise at this point. His views are stated informally and with an apologetic intent. So he should be read generously. Perhaps at certain points he realized that the simple scheme—ideas first, then action—could be deepened. Indeed, in his next chapter, he will start out with a consideration of the unity of the human person.[16] Here, in chapter 9, he relates how he changed his mind about using the word *creative* pertaining to human activity. At first he thought that term should be restricted to God, who is the only Creator. But then it occurred to him that if we truly are made after his image, then human activity is creative, following the divine pattern. There is a difference, but also a parallel.[17] Creativity is richer than simply having an idea and then going into action.

So, why such a consistent stress on the inward origins of every action? Presumably because ideas matter so much to Schaeffer. Also, such a pattern underscores human significance and responsibility. Throughout his work, Schaeffer argued for the significance of man, the reality of history, and the like. Such a theme is fundamental to his apologetics. Here, he speaks of the inward origins of sin, which has the implication, among others, of avoiding any whiff of external coercion. Likewise, he points out that the Christian life is animated because of the Holy Spirit's indwelling (*indwelling!*). Through the Spirit we are compelled by love, which is inward. Even attacks coming from the outside must be dealt with inwardly.[18] All of these emphases highlight human significance.

What would happen in the next generation of evangelical apologetics is a greater recognition of the social nature of knowledge. A pioneer in this development is Os Guinness. As has been mentioned, he was Francis Schaeffer's associate for a number of years. Then he moved to Oxford to do a DPhil under David Martin, the eminent sociologist of religion. The subject of his dissertation was the implications of Peter Berger's sociology for Christian apologetics. Berger has extensively studied the social dimension of knowledge, which is in dialogue with human worldviews. Without at all neglecting ideas, he shows the many ways in which social structures can shape our thinking, as well as the other way around.[19] From Berger, Guinness introduced such concepts as *plausibility structures* and *pluralization* and *privatization* into Christian apologetic argument.

---

[16] *CW*, 3:315.
[17] *CW*, 3:309.
[18] *CW*, 3:310.
[19] Peter L. Berger, *The Homeless Mind: Modernization and Consciousness* (New York: Vintage, 1974); Berger, *The Sacred Canopy: Elements of a Sociological Theory of Religion* (New York: Anchor, 1990).

The first published version of these insights was *The Gravedigger File*, an imagined story in which a senior spy trains a junior spy in the art of subverting the church. One of the chief ways to undermine the church he calls "The Sandman Effect." Christians for a long time have thought that the true battle happens in the mind, and so apologetics must be done chiefly by using the language of philosophy. Guinness argues that the effect of narrowing the field to the rigors of philosophy is to put the church to sleep. People are far more than philosophizing beings. The mind matters, but so do our relationships, the institutions we inhabit, our culture, and so on. Thus the full battle has to include all of these features that define why we think and behave in certain ways.[20]

The danger in the post-Marxist academic world is to *reduce* ideas to social structures. Culture studies today are often based on such a reduction, stemming from historicism. Ideas do matter. Ultimately historicism diminishes human significance and responsibility. But Schaeffer's emphasis is so vigorously against any sort of determinism, social or otherwise, that he may have missed something of the richness of human life. Studies on biblical anthropology bear out that we humans possess a complex set of motives, dispositions, ideas, bodies, social groups, cultures, and so forth. The description of our comportment simply as ideas first and actions second may miss some of that complexity.[21]

### The Circle of Our Existence

Next, in chapter 10, Schaeffer looks at what he calls psychological problems. Still discussing man's separation from himself, this chapter goes deeper into the concept of sin in its complexity. Sin is more than a forensic matter because the truth against which sin offends is more than an abstract truth. These paragraphs are rather dense and they draw a good deal from his notions on apologetics. Distilling it all, Schaeffer argues that human identity ("the question of man") is in two parts: existence as such and the "circle of existence." On the one hand, we exist, and we cannot escape the problem of being. On the other hand, we exist in relation to God. Unbelievers do as well, but they deny it and so force themselves into

---

[20] Os Guinness, *The Gravedigger File: Papers on the Subversion of the Modern Church* (Downers Grove, IL: InterVarsity, 1983). An updated version is titled, *The Last Christian on Earth: Uncover the Enemy's Plot to Undermine the Church* (Norwood, MA: Regal, 2010).

[21] See, for example, Hans Walter Wolff, *The Anthropology of the Old Testament* (Minneapolis: Augsburg, 1974).

an impossible dilemma. Christians, however, not only stand in relation to a God who exists, compared with whom we are finite, but also can have communion with this God, because we are rational and moral beings.[22]

Sin, therefore, is the attempt to live outside of this circle of existence. The judgment against sinners is that even as they try to live outside of the framework where they have been placed, their very beings rise up in protest. Human rebellion takes place in at least two areas. In terms of our rationality we try to leap upstairs, into absolute mysticism. The result is that we separate ourselves from ourselves, since we were meant to be rational creatures. In terms of morality we try to live as though there were no right and wrong. But again, we find ourselves in tension with our very selves, since we have standards, though poor ones, and we cannot even live up to those with any consistency.[23] Schaeffer goes on to develop this view of the separation from the self with various illustrations. His main point is that we are deeply divided from ourselves. Even God's first curse on Adam and Eve was largely in terms of this division.[24]

Schaeffer then describes some of the contours of this psychological result of the fall. He acknowledges that we can learn something from non-Christian psychologists such as Carl Gustav Jung. They are often pragmatically helpful even though they do not acknowledge the Christian worldview. Interestingly, Schaeffer does not use the concept of *common grace* here. I don't believe he used the term much, if at all. However, numerous concepts in his thought are the functional equivalents of common grace.

One of them, already alluded to, made its way into standard evangelical vocabulary: *cobelligerence.* By this is meant fighting alongside someone who shares our concern over a particular issue but who does not agree with us on much else. The shared concern could be pro-life issues, where Protestants and Roman Catholics stand together. Many other issues can be faced together with our cobelligerents.[25] Another counterpart to common grace is the way Schaeffer could build bridges toward other people in discussions, showing appreciation for their insights. Those bridges were

---

[22] *CW*, 3:316–18.
[23] *CW*, 3:318–19.
[24] *CW*, 3:320.
[25] See Francis A. Schaeffer et al., *Plan for Action: An Action Alternative Handbook for* Whatever Happened to the Human Race? (Old Tappan, NJ: Revell, 1980), 68. On Schaeffer and common grace, see the excellent article by Daniel Strange, "Co-belligerence and Common Grace: Can the Enemy of My Enemy Be My Friend?," *The Cambridge Papers* 14, no. 3 (September 2005).

possible because, as he often put it, "we're the same flesh and blood." Yet another way he acknowledged something like common grace was when discussing God's judgments and blessings on human history. As Richard Mouw has pointed out, both Schaeffer and Rookmaaker were helpful in explaining how art and other good things can come out of a fallen world, even if the two men did not always interact with the theological literature on the subject of common grace.[26]

Schaeffer finishes the chapter, again, by distinguishing between psychological guilt and real guilt. Psychological guilt can occur even when there may no objective guilt. Or it can be absent even when there is true moral guilt. Modern people, in fact, try to deny the reality of moral guilt. They try to erase the guilt feelings, but cannot because those feelings arise from true guilt. So the guilty person just feels worse. At the same time, when there is nothing to feel guilty about because the sin has been dealt with, then we need to tell our accusing conscience to get down, and we need to turn to God and thank him. Schaeffer adds that we are very deep persons, and like the proverbial iceberg, nine tenths of our moral life lies under the surface. As we discussed above in the section "Properly Inward," we are still responsible for sins unknown. While we cannot even become perfectly free from known sins, the best we can do is appeal to God when we do know something because it has surfaced, and then ask him to dig down deeper and bring more things to the surface so we can also deal with that particular sin; and so it goes. Fran rather movingly calls attention to the problems and storms all of us have in this life, but insists that with the Holy Spirit's help, we can see "substantial progress" in dealing with the results of the bonds of sin.[27]

### Psychological Well-being

Next, in chapter 11, Schaeffer discusses *substantial healing* in the present life. Although there is considerable repetition of concepts here, they are illustrated in different ways. Again, he makes two basic points: (1) there is the true possibility of substantial healing, and yet (2) this does not mean perfection. This chapter is also steeped in apologetics, as well as very pas-

---

[26] Richard Mouw, "The Uncommon Benefits of Common Grace," *Christianity Today*, July 8, 2002, available at http://www.christianitytoday.com/ct/2002/july8/5.50.html. Mouw suggests that they did not provide any biblical or theological reasons for the love of art, which I think states things too strongly. I owe this judgment to both Colin Duriez and Jerram Barrs.
[27] *CW*, 3:222–25.

toral. For example, Fran discusses the heavy pressure parents can put on their children to attain an impossible standard. We can lose the idea of substantial progress by romantically denying the fall. As he often does, Schaeffer illustrates this with a married couple who refuse to have the beauty they can have in their relationship because they demand too much of one another. As he often puts it, if you demand perfection or nothing, you will get nothing.[28] A frightening array of psychological problems develops because we do not have a realistic understanding of who we are and what we are meant to be. We are neither animals that, like Pavlov's dog, salivate at the bell, nor are we God, able to carry the weight of the world upon our own shoulders.[29]

Schaeffer then discusses the issue of *fear*. Again, using his apologetics, he sees three sources for fear: the fear of the impersonal, the fear of nonbeing, and the fear of death.[30] These are very real in modern persons. And it will not do, as he says Carl Jung did, simply to act *just as though* there were a God when you don't know who he is, or even whether he is. Christian faith begins with the objective reality of God's existence and moves from there to deal with these specific fears. Just as a parent comforts a child crying in bed at night with the thought that the good Lord is watching over him, we can say to ourselves, *no need to fear, because our God really is there.*[31]

Schaeffer also discusses *pride*. Again the pastor, he notes that the same person can experience feelings of inferiority and superiority to others. Both result from a wrong-headed attempt to establish one's validity only in comparison with other people, rather than in the presence of God. Fran wrote these things in a time before the trendy discussion of self-esteem took off, but his insights apply. Whether the attitude is superiority or inferiority, the remedy is the same: be cleansed by the present effects of the blood of Christ, and know who you are.[32]

Schaeffer goes on to discuss "positive psychological hygiene" and "the integration of my personality." He identifies a number of false integration points, the enemies of psychological health. We might call them idols: excessive alcohol, mindless entertainment, and out of control sports, music, art, and sex. He also denounces the idolatry of intellectual pursuits that are only games. Even orthodox theology and church programs

---

[28] *CW*, 3:329.
[29] *CW*, 3:329–30.
[30] *CW*, 3:331.
[31] *CW*, 3:333.
[32] *CW*, 3:334.

can become games.[33] Interestingly, he comments on the exaggerated prevalence of psychology in our time, what we might call the therapeutic culture. Many of us remember how the study of psychology blossomed in the 1960s and 1970s. Schaeffer appreciates the insights that can be gained from such studies. He says, though, that the faithful pastor in a small village who preaches the Word of God is dealing competently with psychological problems even though he may never have heard of the discipline of psychology. Learning from the psychologists is fine, as long as we always affirm the ultimate solution: fellowship with the Creator through Jesus Christ by the power of the Holy Spirit. "Roll your cares upon Me, because I care for you," he paraphrases 1 Peter 5:7. "Come to me, all who labor and are heavy laden, and I will give you rest," is an invitation not only to the non-Christian but also to the believer (Matt. 11:28). Once we see this, we need not fear. God will never cast us away the way the soldier casts away a useless weapon.[34]

### Loving our Neighbor

Schaeffer then turns in chapter 12 from man's separation from himself to his personal relationships, or as he calls it, the problem of separation from my fellow men. In familiar fashion he grounds human relations in the primary relation with God. Just as our relationship with God can never be mechanical, but is always personal, so our relationship with our neighbor should be person to person. Unlike humanism, which "loves" all of humanity indiscriminately, my neighbor is never faceless, but another person. There is a crucial difference between the vertical and the horizontal relations. God will always satisfy my longings; my fellow human being will not. But in a fallen world, human relations can become idolatrous. A marriage can become falsely ultimate. When that occurs, we are crushed and destroyed. But if God is one's first love, then human relations can succeed.[35]

Still, whereas our relation to God is as creatures to the Creator, our relations with fellow human beings is as equals. All those who descended from Adam are "my kind" (see Acts 17:26). This category is as wide as the entire human race. Although the Bible does distinguish between believers

[33] CW, 3:337.
[34] CW, 3:338–39.
[35] CW, 3:345.

and unbelievers, that does not exempt us from loving everyone. Marriage is for all people, sinner and saint alike; therefore we should recognize the fundamental unity of the human race. When we love our neighbor, it should not be conditional, any more than the Good Samaritan posed conditions before acting kindly to the victim on the road. Nor is my neighbor merely an object to be led to Christ. Much evangelism, Fran tells us, "is not only sub-Christian, but sub-human—legalistic and impersonal."[36]

Equality does not mean there are no boundaries. The church needs to respect true doctrine and exercise discipline when some do not subscribe to it. Parents hold a certain "office," which gives them proper authority over their children. The child is both a fellow creature and a dependent on his parents. Fran makes extensive remarks about marriage and the need to nurture rich communication between spouses. Even within the "legal circle" of their marriage, they are truly equals. Particularly, Christians should exhibit the "ring of life and song within the legal circle of marriage." He quotes the Song of Songs, which tenderly calls the wife "my sister, my bride" (4:9, 12). Elders in the church similarly command respect, but this should mean not raw authority but service; not dominance, since the people they serve are equals, but a gentle authority. Schaeffer quotes extensively from the *haustafeln* portions (or household codes) of the New Testament letters as proof that there is form and freedom in human relationships.[37]

Fran goes on to address the question of broken relationships. There is nothing revolutionary here, but he expresses it with great sensitivity. When I have hurt my neighbor, first, I have sinned against God. And, second, the sin may be forgiven. But, third, the man against whom I have sinned is a person, one who matters greatly. However humiliating it might be, I need to tell the person how sorry I am, because it is right. This, in fact, is true communication.[38] And even if the incident that led to hurt occurred in the past, "I must go back if possible, pick up the pieces, and say, 'I am sorry.'"[39] Christianity is beautiful, he says, in that it has sparkling answers to intellectual issues, but also because of "the beautiful quality of its human and personal answers."[40]

The final chapter in *True Spirituality*, chapter 13, is about the church.

[36] *CW*, 3:344.
[37] *CW*, 3:343–48.
[38] *CW*, 3:350.
[39] *CW*, 3:351.
[40] *CW*, 3:355.

We may postpone considerations of this subject, since it occupies an entire chapter later in this book. For now, we can say that Schaeffer speaks in the strongest terms of the need to combine doctrinal orthodoxy with fruit bearing and the need to exhibit the real, supernatural presence of God in our generation. Poignantly, the whole book ends with the finished work of Christ, then the last sentence: "And having come this far, true spirituality—the Christian life—flows on into the total culture."[41]

Francis Schaeffer did care about the transformation of culture. But he always insisted that without "Christian reality" neither intellectual concerns nor cultural responsibility mean very much. As he explains in his little booklet *The New Super-Spirituality*, "God has used the L'Abri books and tapes in regard to the intellect, but they would be nothing without the emphasis on the truly spiritual. They would be nothing without the reality of prayer."[42]

---

[41] *CW*, 3:371. In the appendix, "The Dust of Life," Schaeffer repeats the major premises of *True Spirituality*. And he ends with the thought that every abnormality will be healed and that our calling today is as wide as what the day of restoration will bring (*CW*, 3:378).
[42] *CW*, 3:400.

PART 3

# TRUSTING GOD FOR ALL OF LIFE

# CHAPTER 7

# PRAYER AND GUIDANCE

*But God is the God of the waves and the billows, and they are still His when they come over us; and again and again we have proved that the overwhelming thing does not overwhelm. Once more by His interposition deliverance came. We were cast down, but not destroyed.*

AMY CARMICHAEL

### Prayer at L'Abri

Besides the intellectual content and the warmth of the community, what struck most visitors, including this one, in the early days of L'Abri was that everything was bathed in an atmosphere of prayer. Even in the face of our increasing frenetic busyness, prayer continued to be highlighted. When asked, both Fran and Edith would say that prayer was the very basis of L'Abri. Although there were very few elaborate studies on the subject, prayer was highlighted all the time. And it was practiced.

I well remember my first experience in praying the better part of a half hour. On Mondays, I believe it was, each of us was to take one half hour and concentrate on the needs at L'Abri. We took turns going up to a little prayer room. There we found a sheet of paper with several items listed. A few Bible verses were at the top. Then there were subjects for thanksgiving. And then there were needs. Some of them were financial. Others for healing, or for the conversion of some guest. I started to pray on my knees. The time flew by. Occasionally my mind wandered. What courses would I take next year at the university? Would my friends think well of me? Where

125

was my passport? In addition, L'Abri also sponsored a day of prayer and fasting. This ratcheted the whole experience up. To be honest, I still do not have the patience required for a full day of prayer. But a half hour I can and still do!

Edith reflected more on prayer, at least in more detail, than I can remember Fran doing. He was well capable of waxing eloquent on the subject, as the discussion on my very first night testifies. And he did give a series of sermons on prayer, which we will look at just below. But Edith spent more time reflecting on prayer than did most anyone else at L'Abri. Her chapter "The Centrality of Prayer," in *Common Sense Christian Living*, is but one example.[1] And it is a beautiful example. Here is what she says about the nature of prayer itself:

> What is prayer? Prayer first of all is an expression to God, in whatever form of communication you use, of your appreciation of Him as Creator, of the works He has done, of the heavens and the earth, of the amazing complexity of human beings—physically, but also intellectually, emotionally and spiritually. It is praising Him for creating human beings who are so intricate and complicated, and amazing in their creativity.[2]

Of course, she goes on to explain that prayer is also crying out to God in our need. As is the case throughout her writings, the chapter is full of Scripture.

Edith often talks about "the battle" in her writings. She means something like the cosmic struggle for the coming of God's kingdom against the forces of Satan and his minions. Prayer is really the central confrontation within that battle. All through her newsletters there are pleas for prayer, as well as examples of her own praying, whether for practical needs or for the larger purposes of the kingdom of God, such as the conversion of one of their guests.

To give a sense of this, consider an episode in the Schaeffer's life as parents. This one has a happy ending, although not all the stories do. At one point they were concerned over their daughter Priscilla's difficulties with math at school. She had complained that she could just never succeed in her second year algebra without a tutor. So they prayed. The next day, a remarkable Czech refugee, a math professor, came to express his concerns

[1] Edith Schaeffer, *Common Sense Christian Living* (Grand Rapids: Baker, 1983), 205–29.
[2] Ibid., 206.

about his wife's spiritual needs. Quite spontaneously, Mr. Czerny turned to Priscilla and asked whether he could help her with her algebra. "Show me your book," he asked, and proceeded to explain things to her in a clear pedagogical way.[3]

Or, consider the following episode in *L'Abri*, where Edith discusses a particularly discouraging time lasting several weeks. Money had run out, the children were ill, and workers were scarce. The L'Abri community had its regular day of prayer, and Jane Stuart Smith suggested they have another. All of the half hours were filled. Then in the mail came some good news: there would be a generous gift toward the work in England; another $500 came in toward the need for food; a small group of students arrived from Chesières; and several people became believers. Surely, these events were not by chance but in response to their prayers.[4]

It needs be said that both Edith and Fran would be the first to recognize that the Lord's ways are not our ways, and that while we might earnestly desire that he act in a certain way, God reserves the right, for our own good, to act in quite another. As Fran put it in an interview with his son Frank, the Lord is not like a vending machine: you put the money in and expect the drink to come out.[5]

Edith was, if nothing else, a praying woman. One of the prized possessions in the Edgar household is a two-page, handwritten dedication to us inside the cover of her book *Affliction*. Among other wonderful things she wrote, she assured us that both she and Fran prayed regularly for us and for our work in New England, where we were at the time.

It is of considerable interest to learn that the person who most influenced the Schaeffers, both in their missions awareness and (most especially) in their patterns of prayer, was Amy Carmichael (1867–1951).[6] This remarkable missionary had a special burden for girls working in the mills of Ireland and England. Her most effective work was in Dohnavur, in Tamil Nadu, India, where she served for over fifty-five years, often from a sick bed. She founded an orphanage there and was widely respected as someone who always defended the destitute. She once said, "One can give

[3] Edith Schaeffer, *With Love, Edith: The L'Abri Family Letters, 1948–1960* (San Francisco: Harper & Row, 1988), 276.
[4] Edith Schaeffer, *L'Abri* (London: Norfolk Press, 1969), 167–71.
[5] *How Should We Then Live?*, "Bonus interviews" (Gospel Communications, International, Worcester, PA 19490).
[6] See her influential book, *Things as They Are: Mission Work in Southern India* (London: Morgan & Scott, 1903).

without loving, but one cannot love without giving," a saying that deeply affected the Schaeffers, who supported her and kept in touch with her until her death.

Does L'Abri still pray? It would very much appear so. Here is how a recent communiqué describes their prayer life:

> Each Monday at each L'Abri branch across the globe is set apart for prayer. Normally at Swiss L'Abri we take a few hours after breakfast: the workers rotate hosting the prayer morning, beginning our time together by reading a chapter or two from a book which sometimes concerns prayer, but not always. This reading is to encourage reflection and often shows up in my prayers later that afternoon. After the reading, we present our requests to one another and then pray for one another, for our families at home, for the needs of L'Abri, for the church, and for the world. Lunch discussions on Mondays often revolve around prayer: What is prayer; what does it consist of? Does it work? How do we pray? Why do we pray? Shouldn't we pray for more "spiritual" matters than physical concerns? How does one's view of God's providence affect how we pray?
>
> This past Monday we had a special day of prayer and fasting because our financial situation has been desperate all summer. We went through the morning almost as usual, then we cancelled all morning work crews, fasted lunch, and reconvened at quarter to four to close in prayer together. The morning went really well for me; it was eye-opening; it felt productive, though that word doesn't possess the right feeling because my prayer and study was more listening than doing, if that makes any sense. It was cool to intersperse prayer with study because what I was reading would sneak its way into my prayers, particularly into my confession. From what I could tell, the morning went this way for much of the community also.
>
> L'Abri has, from the beginning, chosen this manner of dependence for her financial needs, and functions on a month-to-month basis. With the money that comes in, we pay our bills first, and then the workers' salaries, which means some months the staff take pay-cuts, some months they don't get paid at all.[7]

We need to stress, once again, that this kind of faith mission is not for everyone. The Schaeffers always insisted that their friends and readers not

---

[7] "Day of Prayer," from *Speak What We Feel* (blog), July 9, 2008, http://reneamac.com/tag/labri/.

fall into the error of thinking theirs is the only way, or even a superior way. But prayer was and is at the heart of the life at L'Abri.

### The Nature and the Urgency of Prayer

Although Francis Schaeffer did not leave behind extensive writings on the subject of prayer, he did preach at least one fairly comprehensive set of messages on the subject.[8] Characteristically, the series is not any kind of practical guide to prayer, even less a prayer manual, with suggested schedules and methods. Indeed, he was always wary of such approaches. Rather, it is an enumeration of the fundamental principles for prayer, almost an apologetic with tie-ins to the rest of Schaeffer's teachings. Much of the series is quite basic, although, to be sure, very compelling.

There are four sermons. The first one begins with the reminder of a familiar instance from his life, one I have already alluded to. One day he asked Edith:

> What if we woke up one morning and our Bibles were changed? What if all of the promises about prayer and the Holy Spirit were removed from the Bible by God himself, not as the liberals might remove them, by demythologization, but really eliminated from the text? What real difference would it make in our lives?

Schaeffer answers that for most Christians it would make no difference whatsoever. The rest of the sermon is an extended argument for the reality and the nonnegotiable importance of prayer.

His first point is simple but central to his argument: prayer and the supernatural are always conjoined in the Bible. In typical fashion, Schaeffer amasses numerous proof texts to build his case. While not engaging in a deeper examination of the texts within their context, and without much use of biblical theology, his arguments have a cumulative effect from the many citations. Each of them reinforces the point that prayer and the reality of God's purposes are always connected. To this end he includes Jesus's baptism (Luke 3:21–22), the Lord's own teaching about the generosity of the heavenly Father, who gives the Holy Spirit to those who ask (Luke 11:13), and numerous examples from the Gospels, as well as the book of Acts and the rest of the New Testament. He pauses over Peter and John's

---

[8] The series is available in MP3 format at http://www.labri-ideas-library.org/lecture-list.asp?s=1039.

plea for liberty before the Sanhedrin, for example, which demonstrates a connection between prayer and the revelation of the Holy Spirit (see Acts 4:25). In the end, Schaeffer affirms that the New Testament community is "built on the concept of prayer."

A second point about prayer in this first sermon is that there is no real difference in the language used between talking to God and talking to our fellow man. That is, prayer is not some sort of special ritual, but simply a conversation. Again, he builds his case on a number of texts that exhibit the use of plain, ordinary language to address God in prayer. A conversation with God makes sense only if God is really there. Schaeffer accuses the new theology of teaching that prayer is valid whether or not God exists, because it can give us a psychological boost. He rails against such a notion. He pauses to describe the parable of the Pharisee and the tax collector (Luke 18:9–14). The one thanks God he is not like other men; the other beats his breast and simply asks God for his mercy. "I tell you," Jesus says, "this man went down to his house justified, rather than the other" (v. 14). The point Schaeffer makes here is that unless there is a God who really can forgive sinners, prayer itself makes no sense. Yet it does make sense, because God is "there," and when one addresses him in ordinary language, he really hears.

Schaeffer gives numerous other snapshots that illustrate the connection between prayer and the reality of God. For example, he cites John 14:13, which promises an answer to "whatever you ask in my name." The promise is reiterated in John 16:23–24, where Jesus has returned and the disciples can ask him face-to-face. Again, the point is that asking something of the Lord is real personal communication, whether we see him or not. The geography of the one praying or the one prayed for is irrelevant. Paul can pray for the Corinthian church, for example, whether he is nearby or far away. And the answers are tangible. Paul asks the Thessalonians to pray for his team so that the word of the Lord may run its course and achieve its goals (2 Thess. 3:1). Paul says, in effect, "Pray so that I may have 'preaching legs.'"

Praying to the Father is much like a small child's asking his daddy to pick him up. It is as simple as saying, "Up, Daddy, up." Of course, the Holy Spirit takes our poor prayers and perfects them; he intercedes for us (Rom. 8:26). This is a precious thought, yet it should not diminish the fact that it is I who am praying, using ordinary language.

The second sermon on prayer seeks to answer the question of "why we pray so little." Here again Schaeffer opens with a familiar illustration alluded to earlier. He then reminds the congregation about his metaphor of the universe and two chairs. Unbelievers live in a naturalistic world (liberals are no different). So for them, prayer is "unnatural." But believers, even while saved, often sit in the "chair of unfaith," which means that the supernatural has no functional reality in their lives. Based on this image, Schaeffer asserts that only when we sit in the chair of faith and are fully cognizant of the reality of the supernatural can we begin to practice prayer as we ought. When we live in the fully supernatural world as it is, then prayer becomes the most natural thing in the world.

Thus, in answer to the question of why we pray so little, it is because we do not acknowledge the reality of the supernatural universe and the way it works. But where do we find power in prayer? By connecting prayer to the fullness of our Christian lives. Unlike so many books and seminars, which want to introduce us to spiritual disciplines or methods of prayer, Schaeffer makes the very simple but most profound point that prayer depends on faith borne out by the authenticity of our walk with the Lord. He is careful to state that our relation to the Lord is twofold. First, we must be clothed in Christ's righteousness (the new birth). Second, we must take care to submit everything to the present effects of the cleansing of Jesus's blood. Again, he cites scores of passages that make this connection. Jesus's own teaching in the Sermon on the Mount illustrates this correlation. He tells us to pray for those who persecute us (Matt. 5:44). But we cannot do this unless we can imitate God's own purposes, including his generosity to unbelievers. Likewise, we cannot honestly pray for the daily forgiveness of our sins unless we have experienced the reality of God's free forgiveness to anyone who asks him, illustrated by our willingness to forgive our debtors (Matt. 6:12). Schaeffer continues with numerous illustrations from various parts of the New Testament.

I wonder, too, whether we do not pray enough because of what Schaeffer refers to as "perfection or nothing." We are reluctant to pray simple, natural prayers because we want something glorious and sublime; we want perfect prayers. But there being no such thing, we settle for "nothing," or for very little. When we consider the marvelous prayers of the great saints before us, do we not think, *My own prayers are so inadequate, why bother?* The cure for such perfectionism is to walk more closely with our Lord, who encourages even our imperfect prayers, even demystifying them, as Schaeffer often reminds us (Rom. 8:26).[9]

Power in prayer, then, is related to the quality of our Christian lives. Schaeffer calls this being on "praying ground." In this second sermon he takes up a number of the themes covered in his *True Spirituality*. He spends a good deal of time on the extensive metaphor of the vine and the branches (from John 15:1–17). Just as a Christian cannot bear fruit apart from his union with the true vine, Jesus Christ, so his prayers will not be effective unless he remains in Christ, and Christ in him (v. 5). Similarly, Schaeffer emphasizes the connection between power in prayer and holiness in life. In 1 Timothy 2:8, Paul enjoins his readers to pray, lifting holy hands, an admonition with plentiful Old Testament precedent (see 1 Kings 8:22; Job 17:9; Pss. 28:2; 63:4; 119:48; Isa. 1:15). Schaeffer uses the image of holy hands to support his view that the power in prayer is in part derived from righteous living. As he does throughout his writing and speaking, he stresses here that perfection is not intended, since it is impossible. Rather, moving in the right direction is what counts.

The third sermon is titled "Faith in Prayer." The principal concern here is for us to cultivate an attitude of dependence as we seek reality in prayer. To make things clear and simple, Schaeffer summarizes our approach to God in prayer as requiring two postures: kneeling and faith. By *kneeling*, he means an attitude of bowing before the God of the universe, the infinite-personal God who is there. Kneeling requires both a theologically correct view of God and a living acknowledgment of who he is. And by *faith* he means trusting God that he will indeed answer. Once again Schaeffer covers a large number of texts, mostly from the New Testament, to argue the point.

A couple of examples will suffice. The story of Jesus's calming the storm, from Luke 8:22–25, provides clues to the two postures we need. In Luke 8:24 the disciples cry out in anguish, "Master, Master, we are perishing!" While their plea is stated in fear, the title of "Master" shows they are kneeling, at least in some fashion. Then in verse 25 Jesus asks them, "Where is your faith?" Schaeffer affirms that Jesus requires the second posture, faith, even though the disciples have very little of it. He then explains that no one has sufficient faith, even in their best moments. But we may still have enough faith for God to answer. Similarly, the story of

---

[9] I owe this insight to the editors of this series.

the two blind men in Matthew 9:27–31 occasions the remark that their calling Jesus "Son of David" is the kneeling, and then their response to Jesus's query about believing he could heal them exhibits the second posture, faith.

Throughout the sermon Schaeffer keeps insisting that prayer is not about liturgy or prayer calendars, but is the fruit of a praying heart. The experience of the early church, as recorded throughout the book of Acts, testifies to the fact that prayer is not only individual but also corporate. One of the most moving segments of the sermon is when he is describing the prayer of the apostles after their appearance before the Jewish council in Acts 4:23ff. Schaeffer asks, "How dare this little minority face the wrath of the religious leaders and the oppressors of the powerful Roman Empire?" It is no secret, he tells us, since they had simply bowed their hearts to the God of the universe.

Where do you get such faith? When your view of God is right, then your faith will just grow. Prayer is living proof of our living belief in our God.

Finally, a fourth sermon focuses on intensity and importunity in prayer. Again, Schaeffer begins with a reminder of who this God is whom we worship. He is the very opposite of an impersonal or "wholly other" being. God is a person. And though he is infinite and thus inexhaustible, he is accessible to human beings, who are also personal, albeit at the creaturely level. With that premise in mind, he employs the usual method of taking us through numerous passages, mostly from the New Testament, to construct his argument.

A good deal of the sermon looks at prayer not only as taught by Jesus but also as practiced by Jesus. Schaeffer cites several places that indicate that Jesus went off to pray in isolation (see Matt. 14:23; Mark 1:35; 6:46; etc.). He is truly God but also truly man, and as such gave himself to a life of prayer. Indeed Fran makes the point that prayer accompanied every important event in Jesus's life, from his baptism, to the transfiguration, to his death on the cross. The content of his prayers made a difference in history. His prayer for Peter to be saved from Satan's claims were answered (Luke 22:32).

Again, Schaeffer underscores the fact that prayer in the New Testament is not primarily liturgical, but simple and practical. Even the giving of the Lord's Prayer (as we call it) was not from an abstract theological discussion, but from an existential question occasioned by the disciples' observing

Jesus in prayer: "Lord, teach us to pray, as John taught his disciples" (Luke 11:1). And, of course, Schaeffer illustrates the principle of importunity in prayer from the story of the persistent widow in Luke 18:1–8. He takes pains to say that while the subject of that prayer is connected to Christ's second coming and the need to persevere, yet the general principle applies to all of our prayers. He then goes over the many references to striving together in prayer, praying without ceasing, and so forth throughout the rest of the New Testament.

### Guidance

The Schaeffers left behind even less material directly addressing the question of guidance. As with the subject of prayer, Edith was more prolific than Fran in addressing guidance. And, again, her thoughts on the subject were rarely in the form of an organized study, but were most often interwoven in her accounts of their lives or in brief chapters in books such as *A Way of Seeing*, *Common Sense Christian Living*, and *Affliction*, where she considers the relation of suffering to guidance.[10] Yet we would be mistaken if we concluded that guidance was anything less than central to the Schaeffers' approach to spirituality. One could say there is a tandem: prayer and guidance. Both were stressed with great emphasis in their writings and in their speech.

One of Edith's constant prayers was that the Lord would make clear what she was to do in a given situation—in other words, that the Lord would guide her. We have already seen several ways in which such a prayer led to crucial turning points in the history of the Schaeffers' work. Possibly none is more poignant than their experience with Franky's polio, to which I have already alluded. Edith tells the story in several places. *With Love, Edith: The L'Abri Family Letters, 1948–1960* recounts it vividly.[11]

The Schaeffers were on the boat back to Europe in the fall of 1954 when Franky screamed out, "Tummy hurts, kiss it; tummy hurts, kiss it." Although he eventually fell asleep, he had two experiences of not being able to stand or walk. When they reached the shore, despite some snappy diagnoses from well-meaning physicians, it eventually became clear that the lad was afflicted with polio. On the way to the Catholic hospital near Monthey, Edith prayed, "O Heavenly Father, keep me calm, let me be a tes-

---

[10] Edith Schaeffer, *Affliction* (Old Tappan, NJ: Revell, 1978), 190–210.
[11] Edith Schaeffer, *With Love, Edith*, 294–301.

timony to these people—but oh, please prevent mistakes." Knowing the stakes were high, she permitted a trusted surgeon to attempt a rather experimental procedure on her son.

The procedure went fine, but then it was a question of whether to engage in a second procedure. God apparently gave her a verse: "The king's heart is in the hand of the LORD . . ." (Prov. 21:1, KJV). If God could turn the hearts of kings, she decided, then he certainly could turn the heart of a surgeon. She lamented her own lack of faith. Her next prayer was, "O Father in Heaven, I do believe that Thou hast complete power. Thou canst turn kings according to Thy will, and surely thou canst also cause this doctor to change his mind about another injection if it is not necessary this morning." The doctor came in and decided, indeed, that a second injection was not really necessary. In the bargain, Edith was given a new measure of trust. As the story unfolds, we find that Franky not only survived his polio, but also was able to regain nearly full use of his legs, albeit later in life. We may never know exactly how the surgeon's experimental procedure worked, but the story illustrates the Schaeffers' approach to divine guidance. They were learning to trust God's ways, however remote from human conduct they might seem.

This kind of special assistance in divine providence was given to Edith, and to all the Schaeffers, not only in the most dramatic settings, but also in everyday circumstances. In fact, one of the more moving chapters in *Common Sense Christian Living* is titled "Continuity in Life."[12] The topic is looking for guidance in order to stay faithful to ordinary commitments and relationships in a world where everything is changing. For someone leading such a dramatic life, this is a remarkable plea for the undramatic! In typical L'Abri style, Edith does emphasize choice making quite a bit. A reaction to the perceived Reformed emphasis on God's governance, or simply a needed emphasis on human responsibility? Whatever the reason, we find her frequently making a case for deliberate, conscious choice, even in the most ordinary parts of life. None of it is meant to minimize the active presence of God.

Indeed, throughout *The Tapestry*, she insists that she and Fran never really had a plan or a vision for their work, but were merely responding to present providences. She often remarked about human finitude, suggesting that it was not only undesirable to put one's own plans forward,

---

[12] Edith Schaeffer, *Common Sense Christian Living*, 64–85.

but impossible. Commenting on the balance needed between a completely sovereign, all-powerful God and human decisions needing to be made, she says,

> The true balance of these two realities is a mystery that should cause us to get on our knees and worship God, not to sit demanding to understand exhaustively nor to pace up and down figuring out a system which squashes out all the mystery so that we feel self-satisfaction, instead of overwhelming worship.[13]

Edith insists, as well, that they never really had any kinds of "signs" or other direct visits from God to indicate what they should do next. This may come as a surprise to those acquainted with the story of L'Abri, since it would appear on the surface that some of the answers to prayer were very, very concrete. By Edith's lights, however, there was no special revelation, no direct guidance through signs.

While Francis Schaeffer did not write in a focused way on the technical subject of guidance, some of his output does cover it, at least implicitly. The sermon "The Lord's Work in the Lord's Way" is an outstanding example. The basic theme of the message is depending on the Lord not only for salvation, but also for the *modus operandi* of the church. Since Jesus told his followers that all power was given to him (Matt. 28:18), the church should look to no other source for power than the Lord. Luke puts it explicitly: "But you will receive power when the Holy Spirit has come upon you, and you will be my witnesses" (Acts 1:8). The church needs to be filled with the Holy Spirit before it can be an effective witness.[14] This filling is repeated, unlike the new birth. There is an existential reality in recognizing our need daily and then going on to serve the Lord. The sermon likewise emphasizes the need for humility.

There are very few practical examples in this sermon. Yet, in his typical fashion, instead of providing various illustrations, Schaeffer calls us both to be theologically right and to stand in proper relation to the Holy Spirit (he calls these *reformation* and *revival*). Guidance, then, can only be claimed when both the theological and the spiritual commitments are in place. The implication here, and in many other places in his writings, is

---

[13] Edith Schaeffer, *The Tapestry: The Life and Times of Francis and Edith Schaeffer* (Waco, TX: Word, 1981), 348.
[14] CW, 3:42.

that the church often conducts its business and programs in the flesh, not in the Spirit.

Schaeffer does supply examples here and there of what he means. In another sermon, he suggests ways in which the church can get its priorities wrong, much as the disciples might have forgotten that Jesus alone was left to behold after the transfiguration. Building programs are a candidate: "It is curious that we can do things in Christ's name while pushing Him off stage. I have seen this most plainly when a church has become caught up in a building project and has moved heaven and earth to complete it." Another candidate is a legalistic approach to the purity of the visible church, where people talk about Jesus, but he is not central. Yet another is a particular doctrine, such as predestination or baptism. Worst of all, I myself might try to take center stage.[15] Proper guidance requires a proper humility.

Like Edith, Fran made a distinction between the extraordinary events of life and the ordinary. He used to tell us there was no need for special prayer over what kinds of shoes to wear, or whether to go to market for food. But occasionally one needed to take out the road map, to pray and reflect and discuss our plans when the issue was big enough. And, sure enough, such times did come up, and the prayer was very intense and very real.

---

[15] CW, 3:146–47.

CHAPTER 8

# AFFLICTION

*What is actually required is an account of evil that acknowledges its ineliminably evil character, and at the same time shows us how it can be overcome.*

GORDON GRAHAM

## Two Rooms

Once again, it is Edith who wrote more extensively on suffering, whereas Fran's material either reflects on it in passing or looks at it more philosophically, and in great depth, as he deals with the problem of evil. Edith's book *Affliction* represents the culmination of her views about suffering and is full of the wisdom of someone who not only thought about the subject, but was often afflicted herself. Generally the book sets forth the contours of a classic, biblical understanding of suffering. Suffering is all too real. There is appropriate mystery when we suffer, as sometimes we get a glimpse into God's purposes for allowing people to suffer, and other times not. But always, God intends our affliction for his good purposes. The gospel is abundantly clear throughout, and the certainty of heaven is given a prominent place. The many examples are powerful and occasionally disturbing, making this no sentimental bedtime story, but a very down-to-earth look at life's hardships.

There is one curiosity about the book, at least for me. Edith imagines a museum in which there are two sections, which she calls Rectangle A and Rectangle B. The illustration stems from a conversation she had with a Mr. Van der Weiden, who was dying from brain cancer. She obviously had a good deal of affection for him and his wife, as they appear as examples throughout her book. After a major operation, he realized that he would never enjoy some of the benefits of living, and he became deeply despondent about the waste of dying. So Edith took out two handkerchiefs and asked him to imagine two rooms in a museum. Each has many different individuals drawn as stick figures, the same ones on both rectangles, actually. The one, Rectangle A, represents answers to prayer for each individual in the heavenly places. That is, it represents how Jesus's death and resurrection give complete victory to each person who accepts him as Lord. The victory occurs in three facets: the initial justification by faith, the day-to-day ("moment-by-moment") victory in "the battle," and the final victory at glorification. Rectangle B represents the very same people, but whose victories are in the tangible, visible world. These victories are not perfect or complete, but they illustrate the way God can and does work in individual cases.[1]

There's nothing particularly controversial so far. The overall point she is trying to make, based on her reading of the book of Job and Hebrews 11, is that we are engaged in a cosmic struggle against Satan, who is always lurking in order to accuse us (and God) of not exhibiting victory over sin and suffering. But the Lord essentially says, "Look, all has been overcome for this person in Rectangle A, and somewhere, in history, there has also been victory for each type of sin and suffering in Rectangle B." Thus the Lord can say, in effect, "See, I have given victory to a person who is going through exactly what Satan claims is a final roadblock: losing a child, falling ill, or whatever the case might be." Although Edith is persuaded that no two persons go through exactly the same kind of trials in life, these exhibit halls in the museum are tangible proofs that both gospel answers and real-life answers (which too are only made possible by the death of Christ) are palpable—they are there to observe, to the embarrassment of Satan.

A given person, such as Mr. Van der Weiden, may not experience the full healing he would like, but (1) he has the reality of the gospel, and (2) someone in Rectangle B has actually been so healed. Knowing this, Mr. Van der Weiden may point to such a person and declare to Satan that he is wrong in his accusation.

The puzzling part of this illustration for me is that these two rooms

---

[1] Edith Schaeffer, *Affliction* (Old Tappan, NJ: Revell, 1978), 67–110.

represent an eschatological unfolding: "I believe that there is to be an historic [*sic*] fulfilling of proof that the death of Christ was sufficient for every
kind of victory needed to make the reality complete."[2] What "reality" is
that? Here and in other places, Edith seems to indicate that every time a
victory is given, something of the "already" (in the "already and not yet")
has been fulfilled. And the overall purpose of it all is both to inform Satan
that his taunts are wrong and to encourage the one who is suffering that
life has a purpose, even when it appears it does not. I once heard Edith
say that when every single type of suffering has been experienced, it is
time for the return of Christ. She rather charmingly added that while she
couldn't find this in the Bible, she just knew it must be true![3]

Francis Schaeffer did not engage in this kind of speculation, that I can
recall, although he had enormous respect for Edith. His was rather a more
theological approach to why suffering occurs. In an interview conducted
by Frank not long after Fran had been diagnosed with cancer, he strongly
emphasizes that suffering should never come as a surprise.[4] Although
there is plenty of real beauty left in the creation, we do live in a radically
fallen world. As he often did elsewhere, here he rails against any cheap
answers or easy believism. It is right to ask why, or why me? But not to be
shocked or surprised as though something out of the blue were happen-
ing. Even Jesus agonized in the garden of Gethsemane before submitting
to God's will for the salvation of mankind.

Schaeffer suggests there are several possible sources for human hard-
ship. One of them, not to be ignored, is the battle in the heavenly places.
Like Edith, and as we have seen in regard to prayer, Fran was very much
aware of the invisible background for events in the visible world. The
series of sermons on the book of Job, which I attended, eloquently made
the point that not all suffering is the direct result of personal sin. Sin
might be the cause, and if so, then we need to confess it and get on with
life. But often suffering occurs because there is an unseen battle going
on to which we are not privy. God is not like a dispensing machine, obli-
gated to make a product available at the drop of a coin. He does not owe us

---

[2] Ibid., 77.
[3] Somewhat in the manner of Leibniz (1646–1716), Edith wants to affirm the need for every kind of sce-
nario in a world made by an imaginative God, a world not yet fully redeemed. Unlike the author of *The
Monadology*, however, she sees God as having created not "the best of all possible worlds," but the one he
has made as perfect, though subsequently invaded by sin. A sympathetic evaluation might point out that
in Hebrews 11, some of the heroes received miracles, and others only suffering.
[4] One place to find this interview is in the bonus material added to the film *How Should We Then Live?*

either explanation or answers as we may have formulated them. Indeed, Schaeffer confessed that there can be something quite terrifying about receiving the answers as we envisage them!

### The Problem of Evil

Schaeffer's orientation, while full of pastoral care, is basically philosophical. Here and there in his writings, and occasionally in a lecture series, he addresses suffering, but it is almost always in relation to larger philosophical or theological questions. In one of his lecture series, he comments extensively on an article by John Hick, the British theologian and philosopher of religion. Schaeffer analyzes Hick's so-called Iranaean theodicy, using parts of the book *Evil and the God of Love*.[5] The lecture resembles a running book review, full of compassion but also sharply critical.

In short, Schaeffer favors the "free-will defense" in the tradition of Augustine. As we saw in our considerations of *True Spirituality*, Schaeffer does not go into detail about the thorny problem of God's absolute sovereignty and our human freedom. He simply states both sides, which may be the best we can do. The apologetic point in his use of the free-will defense has a pastoral edge as well. First, evil is utterly real. The chapter "The Dilemma of Man" in *The God Who Is There* lays out his views as clearly as anything.[6] He sets the tone by saying that anyone who is sensitive at all will be aware that the "dilemma" of man is how human beings are at once capable of such great heights but also of such great depths of cruelty. The only people not capable of such sensitivity are those young enough, healthy enough, and rich enough to be numb to the needs of others. He also explains that the problem of evil is yet another place where historic Christianity differs with the new theology. Secular views are no better. Thus, often when describing Jesus Christ, modern people, like the artist Salvadore Dali, use not the truth but mere symbolism to illustrate not Jesus's actual suffering, but "man in his agony."

In a manner suggestive of Cornelius Van Til, Schaeffer states that there are really only two possible explanations for the problem of evil.[7] The first is that evil has a metaphysical cause. That is, our basic problem

---

[5] New York: Harper & Row, 1966.
[6] CW, 1:109–18.
[7] Van Til typically asserts that our problem is either metaphysical or ethical. See *The Defense of the Faith*, 3rd ed. (Phillipsburg, NJ: P&R, 1978), 158.

is our finitude. The other is that it is a moral issue. If our problem truly is a metaphysical one, then we are without hope, for there is no real way out of finitude, and no real cure for cruelty, because there is no way to identify something as cruel or not cruel. Schaeffer explains that the new theology defines man as fallen man.[8] If there is no transition from original perfection to sinful corruption, then cruelty is just a part of our intrinsic human nature. And this, in turn, means that "God is the devil."[9] But if the problem is moral, that is, if we humans have made a sinful choice, then there can be hope, because that situation can be reversed, and has been reversed, in the cross. Jesus, the man, who is also God, took the weight of sin upon himself and cancelled the penalty.

In the section "The Scandal of the Cross," Schaeffer compares the Christian gospel to Albert Camus's 1947 story *The Plague*.[10] Camus's powerful novel depicts the North African town Oran, which is struck by the black plague. Below the surface level of the story, there is a deeper, theological significance. According to Schaeffer, the reader is confronted with a serious choice: "Either he must join the doctor and fight the plague, in which case, says Camus, he will then also be fighting God; or he can join with the priest and not fight the plague, and thus be anti humanitarian."[11] Such a dilemma confronts anyone who does not have the Christian answer.[12] Schaeffer goes on to argue extensively that the new theology is incapable of giving any answer to the dilemma, mainly because it holds not to the "moral" view of the fall, but to the "metaphysical" view, at least in effect. Nor can it affirm a moral universe, nor a true antithesis between right and wrong, nor, consequently, an objective view of justification, whereby a person can know a real change in his or her relationship to God. He warns against cooperating with evangelistic enterprises that partner with those who espouse the new theology.[13]

---

[8] He may be thinking of Paul Tillich (1886–1965), who is not comfortable with the idea of a historical fall, but who speaks instead of a transition from essence to existence, which in effect does not explain human moral corruption. *Systematic Theology*, vol. 2 (Chicago: University of Chicago Press, 1957), 41.

[9] A saying Schaeffer attributes to the French poet Charles Baudelaire (1821–1867). I have not been able to locate this quote, which Schaeffer uses often. It may come from a particular interpretation of Baudelaire's *Les Litanies de Satan*, in the *Fleurs du mal*, where he invokes the Devil with god-like respect, and even suggests he does a better job running the world than the Lord God himself.

[10] *CW*, 1:110–12.

[11] *CW*, 1:111.

[12] This "dilemma" fairly accurately summarizes one of the main challenges in *The Plague*. Dr. Rieux is an atheist who believes he must fight against the "creation" wherever he finds it. In fairness to Camus's description of the priest, however, it is important to point out that Father Paneloux begins as a moralist who blames the sin of the people for the plague, but ends up deeply concerned about children dying and urges the congregation to stop at nothing in its fight against the plague.

[13] *CW*, 1:112. Schaeffer never cites any specific persons or movements in support of this critique.

The biblical view does, however, provide an answer, because it affirms a moral universe and therefore the possibility of change. Movingly, he explains why *The Plague* is insufficient, namely, because it presents the false dilemma: fighting the plague by fighting God or acquiescing to the plague and giving up on humanitarian efforts to fight against evil.[14] The true, biblical outlook, instead, has us fight the plague precisely because we are on God's side in doing so. Following a marvelous study by Benjamin Warfield, Schaeffer asserts that when Jesus stood before the tomb of Lazarus, he not only wept but was angry at the death of Lazarus, though not against God.[15] "In Camus' words, Christ hated the plague. He claimed to be God, and *He could hate the plague without hating himself as God.*"[16] Within the biblical world of absolutes, we hate evil because God hates it too, as was demonstrated by the high cost of the cross of Christ. However, in a world without absolutes, there can be no social justice. If God is not there, then who decides what justice is? The majority? A tyrant?[17]

Schaeffer revisits this basic point throughout his writings. As we would expect, he makes the same case in the appropriate section of *Genesis in Space and in Time*. The fall of mankind occurred in history and was not in any way a Tillichian fall upward.[18] While Eve's sin began the moment she believed Satan, her fall involved a historical sequence, moving from the belief to eating, then giving the fruit to Adam.[19] And just as she was beguiled, so are we, at our point of history, whenever we sin. Schaeffer does not interact with the theological discussions on the manner of transmission of Adam's sin to the rest of humanity.[20] He does tell us in passing how difficult it is for a man or a woman to resist a potential spouse who is not a believer.[21] But his basic point is simply stated: sin has entered the world. Schaeffer not only points to the many biblical texts that affirm the universal reign of sin (Jer. 17:9; John 8:44; Rom. 3:10–12; 5:12–19; etc.), but also explains that it is easier, in one way, to proclaim human sinfulness than it might have been a few years ago. That is because today artists are

---

[14] *CW*, 1:117.
[15] The Greek word *embrimaomai*, used twice here to describe Jesus's feelings (John 11:33, 38), is often translated as "disturbed," but it really means something like "angry" in the manner of a snorting horse (B. B. Warfield, "On the Emotional Life of Our Lord," in *Biblical and Theological Studies* [New York: Scribner's Sons, 1912], 35–90). The Sunday after 9/11 in New York, pastor Timothy Keller preached on John 11, making the same point, for the comfort of the traumatized.
[16] *CW*, 1:117; italics his.
[17] *CW*, 1:118.
[18] *CW*, 2:57.
[19] *CW*, 2:59.
[20] We do not know if he believed in mediate or immediate imputation, or in traducianism.
[21] *CW*, 2:60.

constantly remarking on human evil.[22] At any rate, sin is universal, and Christians have no reason to be proud of themselves.

> Don't be proud. As you look out across the world of sinners, weep for them. Be glad indeed if you are redeemed, but never forget as you look at others that you have been one of them, and in a real sense we are still one with them, for we still sin. Christians are not a special group of people who can be proud; Christians are those who are redeemed—and that is all![23]

In the same section, Schaeffer expounds on the universal reign of sin. We are all under judgment. We are all guilty; we have true guilt, leading to guilt feelings. Open communication with God is gone, just as for Adam and Eve there could no longer be fellowship with God in the cool of the day.[24]

Human beings become alienated from one another. Using the reference to the woman's desire being for her husband (Gen. 3:16), Schaeffer tells us that henceforth unstructured democracy will never be possible. "In a fallen world (in every kind of society—big and small—and in every relationship) structure is needed for order. God himself here imposes it on the basic human relationship. Form is given, and without such form, freedom would only be chaos."[25] It is not clear from this exegesis whether Schaeffer believed that government in itself is a creation ordinance. On the surface, he seems closer to a libertarian view than to a Kuyperian conviction that government is rooted in the creation order.[26]

Nature itself has become abnormal. This is a point Schaeffer makes throughout his writings, and particularly in *Pollution and the Death of Man*. There he stresses the cause of this curse upon nature. The entire universe is fallen, a condition that came about because of God's response to human sin. God declared this abnormality to come into being by fiat. From this Schaeffer deduces that we live in a universe where God speaks and results happen. It is the opposite of the uniformity of cause and effect in a closed system, another point he makes many times elsewhere.[27] At the same

---

[22] *CW*, 2:61. Schaeffer often commented on artists of his time who depicted a particularly bleak view of humanity. Among the painters were Francis Bacon, Otto Piene, Pablo Picasso, and Marcel Duchamp. He also cited musicians, filmmakers, and poets (often quoting T. S. Eliot's *The Waste Land*).
[23] *CW*, 2:63.
[24] *CW*, 2:64.
[25] *CW*, 2:66.
[26] Abraham Kuyper believed that government, like all other spheres, is an institution embedded in the creation order. Jerram Barrs assures me that Schaeffer did believe government is rooted in the creation order. E-mail message to author, October 30, 2011.
[27] *CW*, 2:67.

time, a world in which God speaks and acts gives us hope. The same God who declared the fall in response to Adam's "unprogrammed and significant" revolt can also give us *Noah*, whose name means "rest" or "comfort."

Thus, while this material is not strictly a pastoral response to particular human suffering, and while it lacks the poignant illustrations found in Edith's treatment of the subject, nevertheless one can easily see how such teaching can in fact bring great comfort to a suffering person. Some may feel that Schaeffer's approach, in the end, is Calvinist and could sound harsh. Some might take umbrage at his insistence on the reality of our moral culpability. But the effect is really just the opposite. The new theology's response and the pantheist response, in which evil is an illusion, are in fact the cruel ones, offering no way out.

Though it is not pleasant to contemplate human guilt, that is a diagnosis far more hopeful in the end than evasions of culpability. Only when we fully grasp not only our guilt but also our inability to heal ourselves can we begin to appreciate the radical and marvelous answer of God's grace. The apostle Paul grasped this when in Romans 7:24 he called himself a "wretched man." His language could not be stronger. He asks, "Who will deliver me from this body of death?," but immediately follows with a doxology: "Thanks be to God through Jesus Christ our Lord!" (v. 25). If we are only a little at fault, or partly responsible, we will neither have an adequate diagnosis of our condition nor be able to grasp the high cost of the solution in the cross of Christ. Behind that high cost is a God who loves even the most destitute sinner. We really cannot have the one without the other. This is what Francis Schaeffer was at pains to tell us.

# CHAPTER 9

# LIFE IN THE CHURCH

*In a Christian community everything depends upon whether each individual is an indispensable link in the chain. Only when even the smallest link is securely interlocked is the chain unbreakable.*

DIETRICH BONHOEFFER

**Observable Love**

Francis Schaeffer had an interesting relationship with the church. We have seen how in the Schaeffers' journey their work was sometimes squarely within the classic denominational church, and sometimes quite independent from it. At L'Abri, while it was never said in so many words, there was a subtext noticeably critical of the church. We are not referring to the liberal church, which regularly received the strongest condemnation. The evangelical church was often the target of opprobrium as well, though in a different way. If one listened carefully, one could discern a critique, not of the idea of the church—for basically, the Schaeffers worked within a Reformed tradition with a covenant theology of the people of God, including its Presbyterian expression—but of the contemporary evangelical face of the church. Still, many left L'Abri, if not with a chip on their shoulder about the established church, evangelical or not, yet with a wariness about it. Accordingly, the church, its problems and opportunities, is the subject of several of Schaeffer's most important volumes.

It is important to say that Francis Schaeffer was a churchman. He tirelessly referred to the church as the bride of Christ. Jerram Barrs has helpfully communicated to me that working alongside Schaeffer for many years proved to him that Fran was very much a churchman, and that it was clear that for Schaeffer the church is the only institution established by Jesus Christ for the whole of this age. Compared with this, a ministry such as L'Abri was structured such that it should go out of existence once its ministry was no longer needed, as should any parachurch ministry.[1]

Some of that sense of wariness came from the L'Abri teaching on reality. Early in his sermon "The Lord's Work in the Lord's Way," Fran makes the following rather scathing statement:

> The *central* problem of our age is not liberalism or modernism, nor the old Roman Catholicism or the new Roman Catholicism, nor the threat of communism, nor even the threat of rationalism and the monolithic consensus which surrounds us. All these are dangerous but not the primary threat. The real problem is this: the church of the Lord Jesus Christ, individually or corporately, tending to do the Lord's work in the power of the flesh rather than of the Spirit. The central problem is always in the midst of the people of God, not in the circumstances surrounding them.[2]

Schaeffer regularly faulted parts of the evangelical church for their "bourgeois" lifestyle. I am not sure when he latched on to this term, but it came up often. Perhaps it was from his work on the Theater of the Absurd, whose purpose was, first, to wake up the bourgeois, second, to tell him he is dead, and third, to invite him to become a mystic.[3] Waking up the bourgeois is a good thing in itself, according to Fran, whereas neither death nor mysticism (the second and third steps) is at all desirable. Continuing his diagnosis of bourgeoisie, Schaeffer sounded the alarm against some of the idols of the church. For example, when describing the "silent majority" of the 1970s, he divides it into two groups: the minority of true Christians, and those who live only upon the memory of a Christian culture, but are more invested in "personal peace and affluence" than in following Christ, come what may.[4] Furthermore, whereas the "old bourgeois" was idealis-

---

[1] Jerram Barrs, e-mail message to author, October 30, 2011. Jerram suggests that I and others go beyond the written texts of Schaeffer's published writings and heed the sermons and lecture series, such as the Westminster Confession tapes, more than some of us have. I have attempted to do that diligently, and still think Schaeffer is sharply critical of the contemporary evangelical church. The reasons will become apparent below.
[2] *CW*, 3:43–44. Schaeffer was here following the work of playwright and drama critic Martin Esslin.
[3] *CW*, 1:251.
[4] *CW*, 4:28–29.

tic and romantic, in the style of Rousseau and Thoreau, the "new bour-geois" just wants a job, a home, and the security of money. Both are ugly, he asserts, but especially ugly is the newer bourgeois to which some of the church has accommodated.[5]

Another feature of the bourgeois church is its lack of concern for beauty. Fran explains that many young people came to L'Abri from doc-trinally solid churches that were nevertheless "Platonic," lacking in any sensitivity about culture and the arts. L'Abri was their last hope.[6] By this reference to Plato Schaeffer means living in the ideal, not the real world.[7] Characteristic of this bourgeois evangelical church is that it takes no risks. Its families will not open their homes to offbeat people who might ruin their furniture. Such unreality is a "cancer in the evangelical church."[8]

L'Abri encouraged nonconformity. While the intention was not to make people suspicious of the church, sometimes, though, that was the result. On the verge of one trip to the United States, Fran urged Os Guinness to grow his hair long.[9] He never did, and indeed the contrast between Os's classic good looks, his double-breasted odd jacket, and Fran's long hair and hiking outfit was striking, even droll. Yet both were after a fashion nonconformists, traveling to speak to the bourgeois church. They meant to preach revolution—not, of course, the chaotic revolution of pure rebellion, but the statement of authenticity amid a compromised church.

It could be argued that people who returned home from L'Abri criti-cal of the local church were principally disturbed because they found such a chasm between those communities and the life of prayer, authen-tic brotherhood, true spirituality, and all the other marvelous empha-ses at L'Abri. To be sure, Francis Schaeffer greatly valued the history of worship and the use of treasures from the past. This explains the prac-tice of singing from Bach's chorales that I experienced on my first visit. Again, Jerram Barrs explains that regular meetings were held to encour-age L'Abri Christians to return home and, rather than be critical, engage

---

[5] *CW*, 3:385–87.
[6] *CW*, 5:388.
[7] Plato (c. 424–348 BC) was one of the defining philosophers of the West. He argued that the ideals, the invisible realm, were more real than the world available to the senses. For Schaeffer this amounts to escapism.
[8] *CW*, 4:95.
[9] Fran told me this story himself. He did so with a twinkle in his eye, but one could sense his passion to reach out to the present generation.

in constructive steps toward the kind of spirituality found in the church in Huémoz.[10]

My own background was not in the Platonic evangelical church. I was already enough of a nonconformist that I did not need any prodding in that direction. But at L'Abri I did meet a number of people who had suffered from this so-called Platonic, bourgeois syndrome, and who felt truly liberated when they saw that things could be different. I have come to think that here is one of Francis Schaeffer's major appeals. You can be solidly orthodox and at the same time enjoy a creative and more humane lifestyle. Besides leading people like me from agnosticism to belief, Fran and Edith rescued numerous evangelicals who were ready to jettison their faith because it was not lived out with beauty and reality.

The charismatic movement appeared to propose another way out of this lifelessness. But Schaeffer was profoundly chary on its type of spirituality. One of his most polemical texts is *The New Super-Spirituality*, a scathing critique of the charismatic movement, along with other similar groups, because of their exclusive emphasis on experience over and against doctrine. They were clearly unlike the historic Pentecostal movement, which, though teaching the second blessing, had a high regard for doctrine, which Schaeffer much appreciated. While it is possible to be too strict, proper doctrine and church discipline are necessary. So is cultural awareness, which Fran found utterly lacking in the charismatic movement. Instead, the charismatics are dangerous. It's a strong accusation. Why was Schaeffer so adamant in his critique of these groups? Because, for one thing, they shared a similar concern with him for spiritual reality as Christians. They were so close, yet so far. And for another, they were not especially different from secular people who had "lept [sic] upstairs."

### The True Church

So, then, what is the church according to Francis Schaeffer? Always with an apologetic intent—no doubt because Scripture always is, and also because the surrounding culture requires it—he identified the church as a "brotherhood of believers." When we take Christ as our Savior, right away we are in fellowship with every brother and sister who has done the same. This, he says, is "the communion of the saints."[11] Three practical

---

[10] Jerram Barrs, e-mail message to author, October 30, 2011.
[11] CW, 2:355–56.

aspects of this brotherhood follow from this: (1) Each member should be of spiritual help to the others, regardless of nationality, race, language, culture, and so on. (2) Members should be of material help to one another. Hospitality, material goods, money—all of these are to be shared, although voluntarily. (3) Fellowship and companionship should be practiced in the brotherhood.[12]

In a word, the defining quality of the relationship of these brothers is *love*. On the one hand, since all people are God's image bearers, we must love them as our neighbors. On the other hand, there is a special kind of love that unites true Christians. Schaeffer sometimes calls this "orthodoxy of community," which must go hand in hand with orthodoxy in doctrine.[13] His powerful book *The Mark of the Christian* argues for such a love.[14] Following John 13, where Jesus washes the disciples' feet, Fran stresses the Lord's declaration that "by this all people will know that you are my disciples, if you have love for one another" (John 13:35). He concludes from this saying that the present world has a right to judge whether our Christian faith is authentic. It may so judge on the basis of our love for one another.[15]

Quick to nuance this approach, Schaeffer does insist that "honest answers" must be given to "honest questions." Wherever we can, we must engage in apologetics. Still, "unless true Christians show observable love to each other, Christ says the world cannot be expected to listen, even when we give proper answers."[16] Not just any love, but "down-to-earth practical love" should evidence Jesus's authenticity as the one sent by the Father.[17] A further nuance is that true love, true oneness, is always conditioned on the holiness of God.[18] Furthermore, if I have offended my brother, I need to tell him I am sorry and move on. This is a very difficult move. It may mean the arduous task of reestablishing contact with

---

[12] *CW*, 2:356–58.
[13] *CW*, 4:33.
[14] Downers Grove, IL: InterVarsity, 1970.
[15] Cornelius Van Til takes him to task for this kind of statement. Unbelievers, who do not share believers' presuppositions, should not be granted the right to judge Christians and conclude whether they exhibit this love and are believers (see *The Apologetic Methodology of Francis A. Schaeffer* [Westminster Theological Seminary, 1974], 48). Van Til admits that the purpose of love between Christians should include drawing unbelievers to faith. But the apostate man is not a judge over the spiritual claims of believers (p. 49). I think he rather misses the point here. Schaeffer is not making a philosophical argument about whether unbelievers have epistemological authority over the Christian religion. He is simply making the informal point that Christian love is part of commending the gospel to outsiders.
[16] *CW*, 4:190.
[17] *CW*, 4:191.
[18] *CW*, 4:194.

people or groups we have offended and seeking reconciliation. This is the more difficult in that doctrine is not the only thing or even the actual thing involved.[19]

There is no better observable love, Fran says, than "saying we are sorry." And there is one thing even harder than saying it, and that is to forgive.[20] As a matter of historical record, Fran wrote to many people he believed he had offended to ask forgiveness, people who were victims of his unkindness before he came to his crisis, when he realized there had been lack of love in his earlier affiliations. Forgiveness is a very deep matter. Schaeffer reflects on the Lord's Prayer, and, commenting on the petition about forgiving our trespasses, he says, "We are asking the Lord to open to us the experiential realities of fellowship with Himself as we forgive others."[21] Schaeffer tells us we do not need to wait for the other person to take the first step. We must have a forgiving spirit anyway, and not only toward Christians.[22] True forgiveness is an attitude, and it is observable. The world is looking on, and thus it can make the judgment about whether or not Christians exhibit substantial love.[23]

### Disagreement

Observable love in a fallen world will inevitably need to succeed in the context of facing conflicts. Schaeffer makes many statements about handling disagreements. He had his share of them during his life. As he lived through various conflicts and often regretted the way he handled some of them, he developed considerable wisdom and insight into facing conflicts biblically. Edith makes the point several times in *The Tapestry* that in the past they were overzealous and harsh. Particularly in *The Mark of the Christian*, Fran focuses on how to handle differences between Christians.

One question is, how can we continue to exhibit proper unity in Christ without succumbing to what we consider to be the other person's mistakes? He outlines five principles.[24] (1) When we have significant dif-

---

[19] CW, 4:194–95.
[20] CW, 4:195–96.
[21] CW, 4:196.
[22] Such a view is not accepted by every Reformed theologian. For example, Jay Adams, in *From Forgiven to Forgiving* (Amityville, NY: Calvary, 1994), 26, argues that we should not forgive another until he or she asks for it sincerely. I disagree. Jesus, for example, asked his Father to forgive his tormentors, "for they know not what they do," and yet they were not about to ask him for it (Luke 23:34). A more recent book advancing this thesis is Chris Brauns, *Unpacking Forgiveness* (Wheaton, IL: Crossway, 2008).
[23] CW, 4:197.
[24] CW, 4:198–202.

ferences we should never come to them without tears and regret. There is a kind of person who rejoices in uncovering other people's mistakes: this person loves the smell of blood. Instead, if we have tears, there can be beauty in the midst of differences. (2) We must measure the seriousness of the difference and act accordingly. If the difference is very great, then we must at the same time exhibit a concern for the holiness of God, refusing to back down, but also seeking the way to show the greatest love in the situation. We can think of the occasions in Fran's life where he was compelled to disagree on basic doctrine with people he nevertheless felt close to. But we can also think of times when he disagreed with people he really did not like; there, the call to love was truly compelling. (3) Real, concrete love may require great sacrifice. Schaeffer often calls it "costly love." We must be willing to suffer loss for the sake of keeping our relationships viable. (4) There should be a desire to solve the problem rather than a desire to win. He says, cryptically, "there is nobody who loves to win more than the theologian." But in life are we here to play one-upmanship or to find resolutions? (5) Finally, our call is to hold up both the holiness of God and the requirements of love. Are we convinced that it is equally wrong to compromise about what is right and to neglect our oneness in Christ? Schaeffer insists that without this balance the world will not know that the Father has sent the Son.

Schaeffer presents two moving examples of these principles in action.[25] The first occurred in the setting of World War II among the Plymouth Brethren. When Hitler required all religious groups to register with the state, half of the Brethren complied and the other half did not. Those who agreed to register had a much easier time of it, of course; however, they found themselves brought closer to liberal Protestants and experienced some doctrinal tainting. Many of those who refused suffered great losses in the Nazi concentration camps. After the war, reconciliation was badly needed. So both groups came together for several days, bared their souls, and searched their hearts. At the end, according to one witness, "We were just one."

The second example involves a church in a large American city where two groups clashed, the countercultural "far-out ones" and the middle-class folks from the surrounding neighborhood. The pastor was unable to minister to both. Finally, they agreed to disagree and formed two different

---

[25] *CW*, 4:202–4.

congregations. However, the elders of the one church worked very hard to maintain representation in the second group. According to Schaeffer, though they had two churches, they were consciously practicing love toward one another. The problem was solved not organizationally but with visible love.

These examples come from contexts where the Christians are fairly unified in their confessions. But what of fellowship with believers who come from very different theological horizons? The issue of cooperation raised its head throughout Schaeffer's earlier days. As we saw previously, early on Fran belonged to groups within Presbyterianism that deemed even other conservatives weak on matters such as the Christian liberties. Throughout his life, he was reluctant to cooperate with Christians who equivocated on various doctrines. Even for the purposes of doing evangelism, it may have to be that Christians cannot always work together. The overall reason is that in an age of relativism we need the opportunity to exhibit truth and antithesis.

> I can visualize times when the only way to make plain the seriousness of what is involved in regard to a service or to an activity where the gospel is going to be preached is *not* to accept an official part if men whose *doctrine* is known to be an enemy are going to be invited to participate officially.[26]

Avoiding confusion, for Schaeffer, included refusing to engage in certain visible platforms, such as praying together, lending one's name to an organization, holding joint worship services, and the like, when there were significant doctrinal differences.

At the same time, Schaeffer developed a concept, mentioned previously, that enabled him to work alongside people he disagreed with: cobelligerence. A cobelligerent is not an ally. Rather, a cobelligerent is someone who says the same things we are saying on a certain issue, without sharing our foundations. Thus, if a social injustice requires a response, and we find ourselves using arguments similar to those used by people who do not share our Christian philosophy, then we may get alongside them and fight the battle together.[27] A counterexample is when the older evangelical, with his middle-class orientation, allies himself with an "establishment elite." This might be an opaque reference to con-

---

[26] CW, 1:197.
[27] CW, 4:30.

servative politics. An opposite misguided alliance is when the child of such an evangelical joins a leftist elite. Yet, the cry we hear, "Stop the meaningless bombings" (in Vietnam), is really a kind of cobelligerence, not an alliance.[28]

## The Message

If the church is a brotherhood of believers who know how to practice visible love, then what is that church to proclaim? Simply put, the church must preach the truth. Schaeffer says this hundreds of times throughout his writing, his preaching, and his correspondence. Of course the concept of truth is prominent in his apologetic works. Truth is often paired with "absolutes" in general, and moral standards in particular. To be true is to be rational (though not rationalist). Schaeffer was so insistent on this that he coined the expression "true truth."[29] Indeed, a cottage industry of books using the title *truth* was spawned by Schaeffer's emphasis, from a number of his own books (and some of mine!), to Nancy Pearcey's *Total Truth*, Charles Colson's *Burden of Truth*, Os Guinness's *Time for Truth*, and many others.[30] Charles Colson was particularly effective in applying Schaeffer's worldview approach to difficult areas of cultural engagement, such as prison conditions. Guinness has tirelessly applied this approach to public policy.

What Schaeffer and his followers tell us is that truth has largely been abandoned in our times, even in the church, and we need to recover it. Regarding liberal theology, things are clear. Liberalism is simply the jettisoning of truth.[31] For Schaeffer, liberal theology resulted from following the trends in secular culture, only using religious language to express them. In his earlier work, he held Kierkegaard responsible for opening the door to liberal theology. Though he acknowledged the differences between liberalism and neoorthodoxy, together they qualify as "the new theology."[32] Later, he added Kant and even Schleiermacher to the list of hinge figures in the development of modern theology.[33] For Schaeffer,

---

[28] *CW*, 4:31.
[29] *CW*, 1:218.
[30] Nancy Pearcey, *Total Truth: Liberating Christianity from Its Cultural Captivity* (Wheaton, IL: Crossway, 2004); Charles Colson, *Burden of Truth: Defending Truth in an Age of Unbelief* (Carol Stream, IL: Tyndale, 1998); Os Guinness, *Time for Truth: Living Free in a World of Lies, Hype, and Spin* (Grand Rapids: Baker, 2000).
[31] *CW*, 4:133.
[32] *CW*, 1:51.
[33] *CW*, 5:374. Friedrich Schleiermacher (1768–1834) is considered by many to be the father of modern, liberal theology. Among other things, he redefined faith as a "feeling of absolute dependence," and sin

modern theology is parasitical on shifts in the general culture, including philosophy and the arts.

So, where and when did things begin to drift away from truth? Generally, as we have seen, these shifts occurred at the "line of despair." In Western history, again, this line represents the shift from a rational, uni- fied field to irrationalism.[34] This sea-change occurred in the nineteenth century. Several key persons were hinge figures in this shift, particularly G. W. F. Hegel. Other players mattered, but Hegel was central because he moved from thesis to antithesis to synthesis. Synthesis in Schaeffer's understanding is tantamount to relativism, in which truth as a statement of absolutes is banished.[35]

Classifying Schaeffer's view of truth in terms of traditional philoso- phy is not simple. It seems he held to a combination of the coherence view of truth and the correspondence theory. For technical philosophers this might be an impossible combination. However, as has often been noted, Schaeffer was not a technical philosopher, but an informal though deep thinker. Coherence entails requiring a consistency of various propositions or conditions. For example, Schaeffer describes a twofold test for whether a theory is true: "A. The theory must be noncontradictory and must give an answer to the phenomenon in question. B. We must be able to live con- sistently with our theory."[36] So, he pleads for coherency, both intellectu- ally and in one's life. At the same time, he argues that there needs to be

as selfishness. His theology and that of his progeny were disputed by Karl Barth and the neoorthodox, although some would assert that they had more in common than either side thought.
[34] CW, 1:57–65.
[35] Like Colin Duriez, I have been unable to locate the exact source for Schaeffer's distinctive views on Hegel and the line of despair (Colin Duriez, *Francis Schaeffer: An Authentic Life* [Wheaton, IL: Crossway, 2008], 41–42). In *How Should We Then Live?* (Old Tappan, NJ: Revell, 1976), 162, Schaeffer draws on his- torian of philosophy Frederick Copleston, cited in James Sire, *The Universe Next Door* (Downers Grove, IL: InterVarsity, 1976), but it is not clear whether Copleston himself saw Hegel as a relativist. Thesis- antithesis-synthesis is a fair summary of Hegel's historiography, even though he may never have stated it in these terms. But for Hegel's philosophy, the key term is *Aufheben* (to cancel and transcend). Schaef- fer was taken to task by theonomist Greg L. Bahnsen, in whose judgment Schaeffer confuses Hegel's synthesis with the irrational (see http://www.reformed.org/webfiles/antithesis/index.html?mainframe =/webfiles/antithesis/v1n3/ant_v1n3_schaeffer.html). A more balanced assessment is by Ronald Ruegseg- ger, who separates two issues: (1) Schaeffer's focus on Hegel's claim that thought is synthetical rather than analytical, and (2) Schaeffer's view that synthetical thought leads to relativism. He argues that Schaeffer is quite right about (1), but that (2) can be questioned, because the final synthesis for Hegel is full rationality and not so much the abandonment of contraries. If such be the case, then Kant might be a better candi- date as the originator of modern relativism, since human experience shapes knowledge for him, although Kant argued adamantly against relativism (see Ronald Ruegsegger, "Francis Schaeffer on Philosophy," in *Reflections on Francis Schaeffer*, ed. Ronald Ruegsegger [Grand Rapids: Baker Academics,1986], 115–17). What might have led to Schaeffer's charge of relativism in Hegel is the philosopher's uniquely dialectical understanding of truth as *becoming*. Although Hegel did believe in truth and disavowed relativism, abso- lute truth occurs only in the "eschaton," when time is removed. Thus every statement of truth along the way is necessarily inadequate, even relativistic. The best study of Hegel and relativism to my knowledge is Daniel Berthold-Bond, *Hegel's Grand Synthesis* (Albany, NY: SUNY, 1989), chap. 7.
[36] CW, 1:121.

conformity to the objective state of affairs, which is more in line with the correspondence theory of truth. Schaeffer states over and over that there is an objective reality. We must live in the real world, "acting on a correlation of ourselves and the thing that is there." Even when we exercise imagination, we can do that because of the objective reality of the Creator God, whose image we bear.[37] We may presuppose Christianity because it "fits the facts of what is."[38] God is "behind" truth, or the "final screen," as he liked to put it.[39]

Schaeffer goes so far as to say that truth must stand before conversion. While this priority might sound strange to evangelical ears, he basically means that conversion is meaningless without the larger framework of truth. Similarly, he sometimes refers to practicing "pre-evangelism" with people. The goal is to be sure certain truths are clear before there can be an appeal to conversion.[40]

It is easy to misunderstand Schaeffer here. His critics tried to point out that pre-evangelism sets down conditions or preliminaries, almost a kind of works-based righteousness, before the gospel could be preached. Actually, what he was trying to do is avoid false consciousness. As Peter Berger once stated, today people are "conversion-prone." We are easily "converted" to this or that idea. Some, such as former yippie Jerry Rubin, have experienced serial conversions. Schaeffer wants to be sure there is enough understanding of the objective basis for the claims of the Christian faith so that a decision to believe is informed and not merely emotional. The ancients expressed the same wisdom when they described three components to true faith: knowledge, assent, and trust.

At any rate, Francis Schaeffer held passionately to the importance of preaching truth. The Word of God contains propositional truth, as he insisted over and over. Speaking the truth loud and clear is the most fundamental call of the church. Preaching truth can be costly. Schaeffer was the farthest thing from an armchair theologian when it came to proclaiming the message. He was truly saddened by compromise of the truth. In the series *Death in the City*, he concludes the chapter "An Echo of the World" in this manner:

[37] *CW*, 1:342.
[38] *CW*, 1:326.
[39] *CW*, 1:57. Perhaps a more satisfying way to look at the question of truth is through the transcendental argument. See K. Scott Oliphint, "Using Reason by Faith," *Westminster Theological Journal* 73, no. 1 (Spring 2011): 97–112.
[40] *CW*, 1:155–60.

I would say to you who call yourselves Bible-believing Christians, if you see the Word of God diminished as it is in our day and are not moved to tears and indignation, I wonder if you have any comprehension of the day in which we live. If we as Bible-believing Christians can see God's Word, God's verbalized, propositional communication, treated as it so often is treated and are not filled with sorrow and do not cry out, "But don't you realize the end thereof?"—I wonder: do we love His Word?[41]

If Jeremiah was a weeping prophet, then so was Francis Schaeffer. It is no coincidence that one of his most poignant books, *Death in the City*, is based on Jeremiah's prophecies. All the while he decries the decadence of the surrounding culture, he weeps and agonizes over the people of Israel. Indeed, his entire approach to theology was deeply personal, and not abstract. In one section of *The Church at the End of the Twentieth Century*, he discusses the way God knows our name: "Christ's death does not leave us with an impersonal relationship to God. Salvation is not merely a magnificent theological or intellectual formula; it is this, but it is much more. The Good Shepherd knows the sheep by name."[42]

### Form and Freedom

Schaeffer was always ardent about the need for both community and freedom. This emphasis involves many levels. Money is part of it. He worries that evangelicals have mechanically limited the sharing of resources to missions or benevolence without seeing the greater need of the community. If love does not deal with the "tough stuff," then it is an empty word.[43] Another part of it is marriage. He chides couples who are merely faithful but don't exhibit beauty in their marriages.[44] The church ought to provide *humanity* for a dying culture. Still, none of these expressions of life is meant to happen outside of given structures.

Schaeffer taught the general principle of form within freedom, and freedom within form—especially in the church. Several spheres of life should exhibit form and freedom. One realm in which form and freedom are crucial is the arts. Schaeffer often commented on the parallel of art to the place of rationality in approaching God. "The artist, to be an artist,

[41] CW, 4:245.
[42] CW, 4:44.
[43] CW, 4:61–62, 65.
[44] CW, 4:62.

needs to be free. On the other hand, if there is no form to his painting, the artist loses all communication with the viewers. The form makes it possible for the artist to have freedom plus communication. In the same way, rationality is needed to open the door to a vital relationship to God." Rationality is not all there is, nor is it an end in itself, but without it there can be no real communication with God.[45] This same rule applies to social structures.

A society without form, as Allen Ginsberg apparently advocated, will degenerate into anarchy.[46] Instead, society needs institutions with basic formal structures. There can be no freedom without them. Marriage is one such institution. Well before the days of feminism's legitimate concerns about abuse of power, Schaeffer made clear statements about how a marriage could go wrong because of neglect of the Bible's clear teaching about a woman's need for freedom as a human being in the face of a man's craving for raw power. The corrective is not to "smash" the underlying structure established at creation. If this structure is undermined, then the entire structure of society will crumble. The answer, rather, is to practice freedom and communication within the form.[47]

What about in the body politic? Schaeffer was not a theonomist.[48] However, he believed that the principles found in the Old Testament civil law could provide "a pattern and a base" for modern countries.[49] While Schaeffer may not have interacted directly with Kuyper, as we have seen, yet implicit in much of his thinking was the need to distinguish the different spheres of society, particularly church and state.[50] He also believed in a rule of law. And he insisted over and over that in matters of government the Bible's realism about human corruption requires a system of checks and balances. "Unlimited freedom will not work in a lost world;

---

[45] *CW*, 1:123.

[46] *CW*, 3:28.

[47] *CW*, 2:66.

[48] *Theonomy* is the term for the movement of Christian reconstruction spearheaded by Rousas J. Rushdoony. In a nutshell, it holds to a greater continuity between the Old Testament law and the new covenant, which in many cases means applying the law of Moses to modern society rather directly.

[49] *CW*, 2:298. The Westminster Confession of Faith sees the judicial law of the Old Testament as expiring with the state of Israel and now providing no obligation other than a "general equity" for our own times (19.4). Schaeffer is less supersessionist than the confession, likely because of his conservatism rather than theological convictions.

[50] Abraham Kuyper, followed by Herman Dooyeweerd and the neo-Calvinists, developed the theory of sphere sovereignty, whereby each unit of society, the school, the church, the family, the state, etc., becomes differentiated since the original creation, and should be governed by the appropriate biblical norms under the sovereignty of God. For a layperson's introduction to sphere sovereignty, see L. Kalsbeek, *Contours of a Christian Philosophy* (Toronto: Wedge, 1975), chap. 10.

some structure and form are necessary."[51] Perhaps his favorite illustration was the one mentioned earlier, the work of artist Paul Robert, particularly his mural on the courthouse in Lausanne. It depicts all the cases coming before the magistrate to be judged on the basis of the law of God.[52] Another allusion Schaeffer made quite regularly was to Samuel Rutherford's book *Lex Rex* (the law is king). The basic concept involves giving a reason for the authority of government: it sits beneath the law, whereas God stands above it. Things go wrong when government attempts to sit above the law. One possible stance for Christians is civil disobedience, although only when magistrates have become tyrannical to the point of violating the conscience of the people.[53]

Form and freedom should specially characterize the church. The institutional church is a visible expression of the invisible church, which includes all believers, past and present. This invisible, or universal, church is what Jesus meant when he said he would build his church (Matt. 16:18), and what the author of Hebrews meant when he spoke of going to the heavenly Mount Zion (Heb. 12:22–23). They point to "the unity of the entire body of believers of all times and all places."[54] But Jesus also addresses the visible church. For example, when he discusses the procedure for proper church discipline, he must be referring to the visible church (Matt. 18:17). When the Lord says about a recalcitrant brother, "tell it to the church," that would be meaningless if he were indicating some sort of invisible entity. Schaeffer points to the church at Antioch as a kind of ideal local church, in part because every social group is represented. That church was the only place Herod's brother (an aristocrat) and a slave (considered very low) could have been drawn together. Antioch was also a strategic church because its members were all "tellers" who felt they needed to send some out on mission trips, as was the case with Barnabas and Saul.[55]

Schaeffer does not interact with the extensive literature on the invisible-visible distinction. Although he generally arrives at the same place, he

---

[51] CW, 3:28.

[52] CW, 1:262.

[53] A full examination of Francis Schaeffer's appropriation of Samuel Rutherford would plunge us into a considerable labyrinth. It is generally true that Rutherford was a conservative who justified resistance only as a last resort. It is not entirely certain that he wielded the influence Schaeffer attributes to him. Parts of Rutherford's view resemble John Locke's approach, derived from natural law, but other parts of it are close to the type of "theonomy" found in some of the early Pilgrims. It seems Schaeffer comes closer to embracing the second strand in Rutherford, even though his conclusions about exactly when civil disobedience is legitimate lack precision. See Stephen Clark, ed., *Tales of Two Cities: Christianity and Politics* (Leicester: Inter-Varsity, 2005), 83–151.

[54] CW, 4:52.

[55] CW, 4:53.

does not refer back to John Calvin's famous *Reply to Sadoleto* (1539), which contains the classic Protestant response to the Roman Catholic view of the church.[56] Calvin argues that there are only three marks of the true, visible church: "doctrine, discipline, and sacraments." Following his argument, Protestants thus recognize, first, the preaching of the Word; then, the rightful exercise of discipline in order to ensure good order; and finally, the faithful administration of the sacraments (of which there are only two, baptism and the Lord's Supper). The Roman Catholic view was restated by Cardinal Roberto Bellarmino (1542–1621), who claimed that the true church is as visible as the city of Venice. Schaeffer would have strongly objected to such a view. Even the contemporary Roman Catholic Hans Küng chides Bellarmino because such a formulation makes no allowance for faith whose object is spiritual. After all, we believe in the *holy* catholic church.[57] The Westminster Confession of Faith identifies both entities, the invisible church and the visible, as crucial for our understanding (25.1; 25.2).

This is not simply a nice theological distinction. It has important implications. Edmund Clowney suggests that respecting the visible-invisible distinction helps us avoid two pitfalls as we regulate life in the body of Christ. First, a belief in the invisible church can mean refusing to require a dramatic conversion or some other kind of visible testimony, rather than simply a credible profession of faith, as a condition of membership. Second, because the visible church is important, we can take seriously its structure and our responsibilities. We could add that if Christ is truly building his church, then there should be some visible results. The church is not a secret society.[58] Surely Francis Schaeffer accepted these principles, but, as usual, he had his own particular take on the use of this distinction.

So then, what are the structural norms that govern the visible church? Schaeffer describes eight places where God requires norms, leaving the rest to freedom.[59] (1) The first of these is that the local church should be made up of Christians. Schaeffer's simple point is that the church is not a building, but a people, with their strengths and weaknesses. (2) The New

---

[56] See John Calvin, *Tracts Relating to the Reformation*, vol. 1, trans. Henry Beveridge (Edinburgh: Calvin Translation Society, 1844), 25–68.
[57] Hans Küng, *The Church* (New York: Sheed & Ward, 1968), 37.
[58] Edmund P. Clowney, *The Church* (Downers Grove, IL: InterVarsity, 1995), 110. It is doubtful that Matt. 16:18 is referring to the invisible church, as Schaeffer claims (ibid., 40).
[59] *CW*, 4:51–60.

Testament local church met, and should still meet, on the Lord's Day for worship. The day is set; the time is not. Always opposed to legalism, Fran provocatively suggests a church should be shaken up by trying to meet at 3:00 p.m., or 10:00 p.m., or even 2:00 a.m.[60] (3) Once the church was established, officers were needed in order to guide the group, and so it is today. In typical Presbyterian fashion, Schaeffer identifies elders as the principal officers charged with inculcating both doctrine and life. (4) Next, deacons were given charge over the resources of the church (he cites Acts 6:1–6). Such a task would not be small, given the challenge of identifying people with great needs and helping them along.

(5) Church discipline needs to be taken seriously. Schaeffer constantly pleads for the purity of the visible church. Without discipline, the group cannot qualify as a New Testament church. One of the themes he spoke about and wrote about most often was the mistakes made during the years when separation occurred from the mainline denominations. One finds echoes of these concerns throughout most of his books in one form or another. In 1980 he gave an address before a group of Presbyterian Church in America leaders in Pittsburgh, entitled "We Don't Have Forever."[61] This is as good a summary of his views as any. Though the separation in the 1930s was right, he deeply regretted the hurts on all sides. Those who left felt judged. Those who stayed felt betrayed. Many of those who left became hardened and lacked love. Those who stayed often became lax doctrinally. Although the hour is late, it is not too late to learn from those days and practice the love of Christ in the present.

(6) Church officers must meet certain qualifications. Schaeffer alludes to the lists in the Pastoral Letters (1 Tim. 3:1–13; Titus 1:5–9) and argues that the church has no right to diminish them. (7) There is a level of unity and discipline beyond the local church, what Presbyterians call Synod or General Assembly. This is based on Acts 15, where the new churches sent delegates to Jerusalem in order to convene and resolve a major problem in requirements for the lifestyle of new converts. The pattern was set: there was a meeting, a moderator, an appeal to Scripture, and a resolution.

(8) Finally, he mentions the sacraments. To my knowledge he does not elaborate on them. Occasionally he makes a passing comment about

---

[60] CW, 4:94.
[61] A reprint of part of the speech is available from the PCA Messenger, Christian Education Committee, PCA, PO Box 39, Decatur, GA 30031. See http://www.pcahistory.org/findingaids/schaeffer/#2.

them, as he does, for example, when critiquing a work of art, such as Salvadore Dali's *Sacrament of the Last Supper*.[62] There is one exception to this minimal attention to the sacraments: his little booklet *Baptism* (1976). The booklet defends the traditional Reformed view of infant baptism, albeit in a fairly polemical fashion. He argues strongly against baptismal regeneration. He is apparently indifferent about the mode of baptism (sprinkling vs. immersion). His principal argument highlights the spiritual and permanent nature of the covenant and, in keeping with covenantal hermeneutics, draws a parallel between circumcision in the Old Testament and baptism in the New. He is cognizant of the church-historical issues, including the antiquity of the practice of infant baptism. He anticipates a few of the baptistic arguments against infant baptism and refutes them rather concisely. I am not sure what occasioned this booklet, but it covers a good deal of ground in a short space.

Schaeffer readily admits there could be more items, or fewer, than the eight he notes. His main interest, though, is minimalism, that is, finding a few rules so as not to bind the Holy Spirit's work in giving us freedom. In part this stems from his apologetics and from the need in our tumultuous age not to put unnecessary stumbling blocks before people.[63] In part, also, it stems from his concern to defend liberty wherever possible. Here, freedom is defined as the liberty to innovate wherever the Scripture does not speak.[64] Again, though, he does not interact with the considerable material on the "regulative principle" in worship. According to the Lutheran tradition, as long as the Scripture does not forbid something, it is allowed. In the Reformed tradition, only what Scripture affirms must be practiced in worship. Of course, there are strong debates on what exactly is set down, and what is left to liberty.[65]

The International Presbyterian Church (IPC) began in Champéry, as mentioned above. The church was founded November 25, 1954 (Thanksgiving Day). At present there are several congregations around the world, and a few others in the making. While the IPC has practiced Schaeffer's eight distinctives, it has also exercised considerable freedom. Only rarely, for example, are things brought to a vote. The ideal is rather to achieve consensus, which means lots of discussion and then a sense of

---

[62] *CW*, 5:188.
[63] *CW*, 4:59–60.
[64] *CW*, 4:65.
[65] See, for example, John Frame's article, "The Regulative Principle: A Broader View," available at http://www.frame-poythress.org/frame_articles/RegulativePrinciple.htm#_ednref25.

resolution.[66] Worship services do feature the nonnegotiable elements, such as public prayer, Bible-reading, singing, the sermon, and, when appropriate, the sacraments. However, worship varies considerably from congregation to congregation. And at least in the beginning, there were marked contrasts with the typical white, middle-class evangelical church. The ultimate hope of the church, as Francis Schaeffer saw it, is that God would be given glory. And in the end, its worship should affect not only the community, but the world around. If worship is real, then community will be real. And this reality will make a deep impression before the watching world.

Schaeffer's critics, even friendly ones such as Ken Myers or Gregory Reynolds, fault him for being weak on his doctrine of the church. They believe, for example, that he was more a populist, stressing the place of the individual, than historically Reformed in his approach.[67] That could be right. Schaeffer's main vocation was certainly in the para-church work of L'Abri Fellowship. Not that he was unconcerned for the church as such. But even when he does describe the church, he does not utilize some of the major traditional Protestant attributes, such as its unity, its holiness, its catholicity, and its apostolicity; nor does he seem particularly concerned with them. There is no question that he was strongly influenced by separatism, albeit in its Presbyterian expression, and did not seem especially motivated by ecumenical endeavors. Indeed, Schaeffer warned the Presbyterian Church in America (PCA) against merging with the Orthodox Presbyterian Church (OPC) when that appeared to be a real possibility. Jerram Barrs suggests that Schaeffer longed for more informal unity and rather feared a union might lead the stricter members to start judicial procedures that would stymie real cooperation.[68]

In the end, though, I am not sure evaluating Schaeffer's work in relation to his doctrine of the church is the best way to grasp its essence. Perhaps the best way to think of Francis Schaeffer is as a revivalist, rather than a churchman. Like his mentor J. Gresham Machen, he judged much of the institutional church to have compromised with the world and its methods. Like Machen, he was one of the rare religious conservatives of

---

[66] One should not romanticize these meetings. They could be passionate at times, and strong opinions could wound. Still, the procedure little resembled that of the average Presbyterian church and Robert's Rules of Order.
[67] Gregory W. Reynolds, "An Authentic Life," *Ordained Servant Online*, available at http://www.opc.org/os.html?article_id=131.
[68] Jerram Barrs, e-mail message to author, October 31, 2011.

his time with a strong intellectual ability. Schaeffer, like Machen, was often quoted in support of antimodernist platforms. In Schaeffer's case, leaders such as Chuck Colson and Jerry Falwell were fond of citing him in support of their conservative American causes. Unlike Machen, of course, he was not a professional academic. Nor did he invest the same kind of energy in the life of the church. Nor was Schaeffer as consistent a libertarian as Machen. For example, Machen opposed Prohibition and school prayer, positions that put him at odds with many conservative Presbyterians in his day. He also was uncomfortable with the label fundamentalist, which Schaeffer was not.[69]

Although Schaeffer cared in his own way about the church and addressed various church bodies, his main influence was as an evangelist, at first mostly based in Switzerland, and then traveling all over the world. The community life of L'Abri was fundamentally important to the entire project of speaking the historic Christian position into the twentieth century and beyond. One can note the development of any number of community-based apologetics enterprises today. It is hard to imagine they are not in some way inspired by the L'Abri model. Take, for example, the Damaris Trust, in Great Britain. While its community is global more than local, nevertheless it combines engagement with culture with resources that put people in touch with one another. Their mission statement is clear: "To build a global community of people who have a firm grasp of the Bible, a clear understanding of contemporary popular culture, and the ability to connect one to the other."[70]

---

[69] "Fighting the Good Fight: A Brief History of the Orthodox Presbyterian Church," available at http://www.opc.org/books/fighting/pt1.html.
[70] http://www.damaris.org/cm/damaris/vision.

CHAPTER 10

# ENGAGING THE WORLD

*So where did we come from? This is the most crucial question humans can raise, because the answer not only determines what it means to be human and why we are here, but it also affects every area of human endeavor.*

CHARLES COLSON

## Cultural Awareness

How, then, are Christians to make their an impact on culture? Let us start with a simple observation. Before we explore the various contours of Francis Schaeffer's approach to cultural engagement, it is worth pointing out that his very emphasis on culture, be it the arts, or science, or politics, constituted a fresh way of looking at things, at least for the average evangelical. You cannot read very far, or listen too long, before Schaeffer illustrates a point from culture. Even when he is illustrating a negative point, you can tell Fran has spent time contemplating and enjoying some art object or some special poem. For example, as he describes the relentless march of the Romans across Europe, bringing their harsh yoke to press down on the necks of Helvetians, Gauls, and Britons, he mentions Aventicum (or Avenches), the ancient Helvetian capitol. "I love Avenches," he tells us. "It contains some of my favorite Roman ruins north of the Alps."[1] Or when he is considering the poetry of T. S. Eliot, you can tell Schaeffer pored over this remarkable verse. He praises Eliot, who deserves

---

[1] *CW*, 5:87.

"high marks" for conforming the structure of his poetry to the content. He even sees an evolution in the form, from the earlier work "The Waste Land" to his later, more Christian poetry. Schaeffer argues that Eliot modified the form of his poems after his conversion. He sees it in Eliot's "Journey of the Magi." At the same time, in Schaeffer's view, Eliot does not return nostalgically to the older formal structures used, say, by Alfred, Lord Tennyson.[2] Undoubtedly more of a visual person than an aural one, Fran nevertheless enjoyed music. He claimed to have "worn the grooves off" his recording of Handel's *Dettingen Te Deum*.[3]

I can remember visiting with Fran in his favorite little annex upstairs. There usually were art books opened to masterpieces by Picasso, Cézanne, Vermeer, and others. His critics thought he was basically showing off. I think otherwise. He was simply more comfortable with such works in the room. And also, we could quite naturally turn the conversation to one of those reproductions and think about the particulars of what the artist was saying. Although Fran had been much encouraged in his study of the arts by his friend Hans Rookmaaker, in fact, as I argued above, he had been fascinated with art and culture from the beginning quite on his own.

One of his heartaches with the contemporary evangelical church was its ignorance, or even its disdain, for such things. Fran recounts taking a group of American missionaries in Italy around Florence. One of the joys of L'Abri in the early days was being escorted to the great Renaissance sites in Italy by Schaeffer or Rookmaaker and literally having our eyes opened to the wonders of these great works, all explained from a Christian worldview. The group stood before Botticelli's *Birth of Venus*, contemplating its sheer beauty. Apparently one of the missionaries asked, "What's beautiful about it?" Fran, obviously exasperated, was at a loss for words.[4]

He often remarked on environmental issues. Most of the time his concern was aesthetic rather than ecological. He hated the power plant on the other side of the valley from L'Abri, because it stood out like a sore thumb, injuring the lovely contours of the Swiss Alps. In *Pollution and the Death of Man* (one of my favorite books—so prescient, and with such a call to beauty), he compares a couple of "Christian" communities with pagan ones. Christian communities can be orthodox in doctrine, yet greatly insensitive to God's creation. Schaeffer cites the Dutch Black-Stocking

[2] *CW*, 2:407.
[3] *CW*, 2:388–89.
[4] *CW*, 3:388.

Calvinists, who are supposedly purely orthodox and yet treat their animals poorly because they have no souls and won't be in heaven.[5] He recounts going to visit a hippie community in California and being impressed with the beauty of the way they treated their quarters, even though it was quite pagan in its views. To boot, as they looked across the ravine, they saw a Christian school that was simply ugly.[6]

The Schaeffers were against plastic! In Les Mélèzes everything had to be natural, organic, authentic. There were real paintings and real photographs on the walls. While there were the odd reproductions of paintings around, they had to be Rembrandts! The furniture was handmade. Decorations included mosses and flowers Edith had gathered on her walks. Edith was a health-food devotee. She inculcated in her younger followers a love for garden-grown vegetables, with no artificial components. Tomatoes were fresh, and cut thinly. Brewer's yeast was recommended (although it is ghastly stuff!). Fabrics were to be exceptional, preferably handmade, whether materials for skirts or textiles for blankets or curtains. In retrospect, this had the marks of a sort of folk culture about it.

Edith was particularly insistent on "hidden art" and spent her apparently inexhaustible energy on hiding presents for her children, making treasure-hunts that ended up in a bubble bath, preparing flannelgraph Bible lessons, decorating tables, drawing pictures for young ones, sneaking vitamins into Fran's food, and so on.[7] Some visitors felt under pressure from all this. But to the hundreds who came up the mountain to L'Abri, a number of them from backgrounds with little interest in culture, it was all quite wonderful.

### Revolutionary Christianity

Francis Schaeffer's approach to engaging the world is not easy to label. Clearly, his entire work was geared to show how a positive impact on culture and society results when there is a biblically based mentality present; similarly, things go terribly awry when that foundation is absent. We may not find any kind of focused academic study of cultural change in

---

[5] *CW*, 5:23.
[6] *CW*, 5:24.
[7] I always resented the change in the title of her marvelous book *Hidden Art* to *The Hidden Art of Homemaking* (Carol Stream, IL: Tyndale House, 1985). "Homemaking" sounds cutesy, even demeaning, for something that really does qualify as art. Similarly, the cover art of the newest edition of *What Is a Family?* is dreadfully sentimental.

Schaeffer's output, such as those studies initiated by sociologist Robert Nisbet.[8] Schaeffer does anticipate the work of scholars such as Malcolm Gladwell, who carefully analyzed the notion of a cultural consensus.[9] The difficulty is that when we try to discern a framework in Schaeffer's work or a model whereby such cause-and-effect exists, we cannot find a recognizable one. Schaeffer did not spend much time with theory. My best guess is that he had a rather classical view, which, as we have seen, is appropriately summed up as "ideas have consequences." We saw in chapter 6 above how this dynamic characterizes his approach to the Christian life. Throughout his comprehensive study of the rise and fall of Western culture, *How Should We Then Live?*, the notion is clearly articulated to the effect that the thought world comes first, followed by cultural and social consequences. Schaeffer states it eloquently in the very first paragraph:

> There is a flow to history and culture. This flow is rooted and has its well-spring in the thoughts of people. People are unique in the inner life of the mind—what they are in their thought-world determines how they act. This is true of their value systems and it is true of their creativity. It is true of their corporate actions, such as political decisions, and it is true of their personal lives. The results of their thought-world flow through their fingers or from their tongues into the external world. This is true of Michelangelo's chisel, and it is true of a dictator's sword.[10]

Does that mean there was no place for the heart in his approach? I don't think so. As he develops this view, Schaeffer emphasizes the role of presuppositions. They may signify something like the commitment of the human heart, which is much more than just an idea. He defines *presuppositions* in several places. For the most part a presupposition is the way a person looks at life—a worldview, or a grid through which someone sees the world.[11] Although he never enters into discussion with contemporary schools—such as Berger's sociology of knowledge, the Frankfort School, or the Birmingham School in the United Kingdom, all of which have mapped out the complex ways in which ideas and culture relate—he would no

---

[8] For example, Robert A. Nisbet, *Social Change and History: Aspects of the Western Theory of Development* (New York: Oxford University Press, 1970).

[9] For example, Schaeffer does suggest in several places that if 20 percent of the population is truly Christian, that would be enough to effect a considerable influence (*CW*, 4:35). See Malcolm Gladwell, *The Tipping Point: How Little Things Can Make a Big Difference* (Boston: Little, Brown, 2000).

[10] *CW*, 5:83.

[11] *CW*, 1:6–8, 345; 5:83.

doubt agree broadly that culture is produced by many factors, not just ideas. At the same time, he would repudiate any implication that ideas can somehow be purely the results of social conditions.[12]

Although I agree with Colin Duriez that Schaeffer generally belongs to the Kuyperian tradition, Schaeffer emphasizes ideas and the rational process in a way that contrasts somewhat with Kuyper. For example, discussing presuppositions, Schaeffer says that most people "catch" them as a child might catch the measles. "But people with more understanding realize that their presuppositions should be chosen after a careful consideration of what world-view is true." He thus points to the primacy of a rational process and choice making. The heart is involved, but much attention is given to the rational mode. He then specifies that there are three "lines" in history: the philosophic, the scientific, and the religious. Clearly, the "philosophic" is first, seeking the intellectual answers to the basic questions of life. Then come science and technology. Finally, "People's religious views also determine the direction of their individual lives and of their society."[13] Here, religion appears to be almost an appendix to what really matters.

For Abraham Kuyper, by contrast, the religious is the most central motive characterizing the human being.[14] Some issues of terminology may be involved, but there is more. For Kuyper the religious dimension is equivalent to the faith component of a human being, whereas for Schaeffer the "philosophic" line comes first. It translates into thinking, the rational process, basic ideas. Surely there is a faith component to ideas for him, but ideas or concepts are basic, to the point where the term "religious" probably means something like theology, which lags behind philosophy and other cultural entities.

Furthermore, for Kuyper, the "cultural mandate" is far more central than it seems to be for Schaeffer.[15] Of course, as already mentioned,

---

[12] To be fair, Schaeffer here and there acknowledges the social factors in shaping ideas. At times he can sound like Thomas Kuhn, who emphasized "paradigm shifts" in the history of science. Schaeffer's account of the movements in Western history from the Greeks ("form/matter") through the medievals ("nature/grace") to the moderns ("nature/freedom") in *Escape from Reason* bear a certain resemblance to the structuralists' notions of culture shaping. He recognizes that some element of conditioning can contribute to human life, as long as it does not explain "what people are in their totality" (*CW*, 5:230).
[13] *CW*, 5:84.
[14] See Abraham Kuyper, "Calvinism and Religion," in *Lectures on Calvinism* (Grand Rapids: Eerdmans, 1943), 41–76. For many theologians, *religion* is a negative term juxtaposed with biblical Christianity. For example, for Timothy Keller, religion is pharisaical and has been done away with by Jesus Christ; see *King's Cross: The Story of the World in the Life of Jesus* (New York: Dutton, 2011), 47. The same is true for C. S. Lewis and Karl Barth.
[15] Although Kuyper did not use the terms *culture* or *cultural mandate* (he thought those implied humanism) the expression *common grace*, which he did use, was their equivalent. It is Klaas Schilder who likely introduced the expression *cultural mandate* into the vocabulary. See N. H. Gootjes, "Schilder on Christ

Schaeffer acknowledges the cultural mandate, at least in principle. In his studies on Genesis, after describing the creation of man as God's image bearer, he devotes several paragraphs to man's call to have dominion over the creation. He mentions Adam's role of naming the animals, as well as dressing and keeping the garden. He mentions the divine ordinance of marriage, though not the ordinance of labor. He even quotes Psalm 8, which is a reiteration of the cultural mandate. He also cites Psalm 115:16, which delineates those places that belong strictly to God, such as the heavens, and those that have been given to the children of men, that is, the earth.[16] Once again, we could think of the book *Pollution and the Death of Man*, which is full of allusions to a gentle human lordship over the creation, one that avoids both extremes of pantheism and scientific imperialism. Still, as mentioned, Schaeffer does not appear to define history and the march of the human race in terms of the cultural mandate.[17]

How, then, does the Christian faith affect culture? First, when the right Christian ideas are in place, then there can be cultural and social improvement. Once again, this view puts ideas first and action as the result of the ideas. Behavior matters as well, of course. At the heart of it, we need "revolutionary Christianity."[18] If that is present, then things can change.

What are the characteristics of revolutionary Christianity? First, it needs to be *hot*. Schaeffer borrows this jargon from Marshall McLuhan. An early scholar of media theory, McLuhan spoke of "hot communication" as the content and "cool communication" as the subliminal message carried by the medium, rather than the message itself. Thus, for McLuhan, for example, television shapes the content of a particular message by its very form: a small square box in the living room, with programs punctuated by commercials, forces the content to be driven by the values of entertainment, rather than simply ideas. McLuhan's work on advertising was among the first to point out how images influence us more than words. For example, in *The Mechanical Bride* he looks at a number of adverts he collected from various magazines. He argues that these ads often disconnect space and time from simple location in order to give the image its power. Instead, they present fragments in a pastiche style, which com-

---

and Culture," in *Always Obedient: Essays on the Teachings of Dr. Klaas Schilder*, ed. J. Geertsema (Phillipsburg, NJ: P&R, 1995), 37.

[16] *CW*, 2:34.

[17] Herman Dooyeweerd does connect the two; see *A New Critique of Theoretical Thought*, vol. 2 (Philadelphia: Presbyterian and Reformed, 1958), 266.

[18] *CW*, 4:87.

municates more subliminally than linearly. For example, an advertisement for Berkshire Stockings is like a Picasso painting, he says, because it withholds syntactical connections. Another is an ad for beauty creams that hawks them as "The Famous DuBarry Success Course," complete with academic-sounding characteristics, such as "tuition." Instead of telling you how nice your skin will be if you use the products, the ad gives the impression that if you buy them, you'll be right up there with the brightest students at our schools.[19]

So, then, Schaeffer chooses to favor not the cool communication touted by McLuhan, but its opposite: "I would like to reverse this. In a day of increasingly cool communication, biblical Christianity must make it very plain that it will deal only with hot communication. Biblical Christianity rests upon content, factual content."[20] Schaeffer is ever the defender of space-time-historical Christian faith, one that is expressed in verifiable, propositional truth: "It is a time for the church to insist, as a true revolutionary force, that there is truth."[21]

Second, revolutionary Christian faith must be *compassionate*. Schaeffer felt quite strongly about racial issues. Although he did not often address them in print, he was deeply concerned for racial equality and made sure that L'Abri never put up any kinds of racial or ethnic barriers in the community. In a rare printed statement on race, Schaeffer laments the white persons' lack of care for black people. He faults whites for not applying the principles of social justice or granting the benefits of theological education to black persons, particularly pastors. In a prescient manner, Schaeffer argues that, had whites exercised proper compassion, not only would the black community be far better off, but the white community would not be "in the place we are now."[22]

At the same time, using what would today qualify as somewhat outmoded race theory, Schaeffer presents an example: whites, he says, had looked upon Harlem as "the poor man's Paris," a place where they could enjoy promiscuous sex, but in the process ignored black people as people.[23] He contrasts this compassionless white approach with L'Abri, where,

---

[19] Marshall McLuhan, *The Mechanical Bride: Folklore of Industrial Man* (New York: Vanguard, 1951), 80, 152.
[20] CW, 4:88.
[21] CW, 4:89.
[22] CW, 4:90.
[23] It is unclear how much Schaeffer really knew about Harlem, either in his own day or earlier during the so-called Harlem Renaissance period in the 1920s and '30s. He would not be alone in grouping all of black urban culture as a single phenomenon characterized mostly by poverty and its discontents, nor in reproaching whites for viewing black culture as exotic rather than in need of compassion. Contem-

though, "far from perfect," people from all kinds of backgrounds appeared, coming to church in blue jeans, with bare feet, to test them out, as it were, to see if they could really be accepted just as people. Surely, this approach to racial reconciliation is a bit dated, missing the deeper dimensions of undoing the "colonization of the mind" and other subtle structures of oppression. At the same time, compared with what was going on in the larger evangelical community, it was innovative. The African American Sylvester Jacobs, mentioned earlier, who provided the marvelous photo journal *Portrait of a Shelter,* will testify to Francis Schaeffer's righteous anger over institutional racism in the United States, even in the late 1960s.

Schaeffer becomes rather irate as he dares his readers to practice community by opening their homes. "I dare you," he shouts:

> I dare you in the name of Jesus Christ. Do what I am going to suggest. Begin by opening your home for community.
>
> I have seen white evangelicals sit up and clap their heads off when black evangelicals get up and talk at conference times. How they clap! That's nice, because twenty years ago the evangelicals would not have been clapping. But I want to ask you something if you are white. In the past year, how many blacks have you fed at your dinner table? How many blacks have felt at home in your home? And if you haven't had any blacks in your home, shut up about the blacks.[24]

In another case, he tells of a man who had a special burden for "the blacks" and asked the church to adjust its service time so that African American children, who had stayed up late, as ghetto culture required, could more easily attend. Of course, the church would not, and instead, "the roof fell in."[25] I suppose it is easy to look at such statements in hindsight and discern latent paternalism. What evangelicals have learned since is that minorities need justice and empowerment, not only accommodation. No doubt the Schaeffers were ahead of their times for simply regarding African Americans as people. Were they altogether unaware of issues such as authority, access to power, partnership in ministry, and all

---

porary black urban culture is in fact a hybrid "that draws on Afro-diasporic traditions, popular culture, the vernacular of previous generations of Southern and Northern black folk, new and old technologies, and a whole lot of imagination," as Robin D. G. Kelley puts it in "Check the Technique," in *In Near Ruins: Cultural Theory at the End of the Century,* ed. Nicholas B. Dirks (Minneapolis: University of Minnesota Press, 1998), 59.
[24] *CW,* 4:92. In fairness, he adds that blacks should similarly welcome whites.
[25] *CW,* 4:94.

of the components of racial justice and racial reconciliation that are now common parlance? Perhaps so. In any case, they no doubt contributed to moving things forward in their own way.

At any rate, revolutionary Christianity starts in the church. "The church has a place," he avers, "but not if it ossifies."[26] By assigning the church *a* place, rather than *the* place, perhaps Schaeffer is looking at kingdom work as wider or broader than the institutional church. Still, he warns the church that unless it prepares for the issues of the day, it will never be ready for its trials. The church is about to be "squeezed in a wringer." There will be revolution and repression, and by the time his grandchildren grow up, we will be in an entirely different culture.[27]

## Revival and Reformation

Schaeffer often talked of the need for both revival and reformation. Sometimes he used these terms synonymously. Revivals in various countries such as Great Britain, Scandinavia, Wales, and others called not only for personal salvation, but also for social action.[28] Schaeffer cited John Wesley's and George Whitefield's revivals as producing very significant social improvements. For example, when the urban poor were cruelly affected by industrialization, the Wesleyan revivals were able to open dispensaries (for medical supplies), schools, and orphanages. Not only did Wesley offer the gospel of free grace, but he also set forth creative economic alternatives to the lifestyles of the new converts. Similarly, Lord Shaftesbury and William Wilberforce were mightily used to eradicate social evils, particularly slavery, long before abolition in the United States. Following the historian J. H. Plumb, Schaeffer liked to claim that had there been no Wesleyan revival in England, there would have been the equivalent to the devastating French Revolution.[29]

At other times, the concept of reformation apparently referred to a deeper, more permanent kind of transformation than revival. Indeed, "reformation" is about the transformation of culture.[30] Reformation is both a historical reality (as it was in the case of the Protestant Reformation of the sixteenth century) and an ideal to be followed. When

---

[26] *CW*, 4:66, 68.
[27] *CW*, 4:69.
[28] *CW*, 5:451.
[29] *CW*, 5:145, 452.
[30] *CW*, 1:220.

the Reformation mentality was strong, then the law of God informed every part of the creation. Such a mentality is not a theocracy, but a consensus in which the law of God is respected.[31] Schaeffer spoke in generalities. His was not the careful work of a professional historian, but rather the more prophetic work of the passionate preacher. According to his view, the Protestant Reformation largely occurred in the north, whereas the Renaissance, in many ways its opposite, occurred in the south. The Protestant Reformation gave us democracy, with its system of checks and balances.[32] The Renaissance gave us humanism, with its eventual destructive tendencies.[33]

Although recognizing that the Protestant Reformation was not a golden age, Schaeffer attributes many cultural and social benefits to its impetus: "So the Reformation's preaching of the Gospel brought forth two things which were secondary to the central message of the Gospel but nonetheless were important: an interest in culture and freedom in society and government."[34] This is a telling statement. While he recognizes the impact of the gospel on at least these two areas, he does not see them as requiring one another. Particularly since the Lausanne Covenant (1974), evangelicals have increasingly recognized the transformation of society as a crucial part of the gospel itself. When Jesus announced to the synagogue in Nazareth that the Jubilee had come, he included the preaching of the gospel to the poor, liberty to the captives and the oppressed, and recovery of sight to the blind, all of them part of the same reality (Luke 4:16–20).[35]

In no way is this intended to downplay what Schaeffer actually has accomplished. His burden was to demonstrate to anyone who would care to listen how much benefit can come when the Christian worldview is accepted. We might remember that he had a great zeal to enlighten the evangelicals who seemed indifferent to anything but the preaching of a gospel as life insurance for the future, rather than as a reality for today. He also, as we will recall, was attempting to challenge the humanistic histori-

---

[31] CW, 1:261–62; 2:298–300.
[32] CW, 3:30.
[33] CW, 5:120. For his views on the Renaissance, Schaeffer is quite dependent on Jacob Burckhardt, whose The Civilization of the Renaissance in Italy (1860; New York: Phaedon, 1952) did indeed set the tone for Renaissance studies for generations. Burckhardt's radical contrast between the Renaissance and the Reformation no longer holds for most historians. See Peter Burke, The Renaissance (New York: Palgrave-Macmillan, 1997).
[34] CW, 5:139.
[35] On the interrelation of preaching and social transformation, see Harvie M. Conn, Evangelism: Doing Justice and Preaching Grace (Phillipsburg, NJ: P&R, 1992).

ography of Kenneth Clark and others who interpreted civilization entirely in terms of human achievement.

In any case, in Schaeffer's view, countries that adopted the Protestant Reformation enjoyed cultural and civic benefits. First, they produced great music, including that of Heinrich Schütz, Dietrich Buxtehude, G. F. Handel, and J. S. Bach, as well as great visual art, such as that of the later Albrecht Dürer, and of course the Dutch painters of the seventeenth century, culminating in Rembrandt.[36] In passing, I should add, Schaeffer makes the comment that painting with beauty is not the exclusive province of Christians, but of any skilled artist made in God's image.[37] Though not a full statement of common grace, this is fairly close. Second, in the social realm, the Protestant Reformation brought "freedom without chaos."[38] Reformation countries generally enjoyed greater freedom because they accepted law, rather than tyrants, as their ultimate authority.[39]

Interestingly, Schaeffer believes, there were two major lacuna in these Reformation countries: race and the compassionate use of wealth.[40] Slavery is a great blight. It represents a "twisted view of race," which could have been avoided. Today we can only hope to work for redress by carefully following what Scripture prescribes in race relations.[41] Similarly, the lack of a compassionate use of wealth dates back to the industrial revolution. While strongly eschewing socialism, Schaeffer maintains that neglect of proper distribution of the wealth accumulated at the industrial revolution is a type of utilitarianism that still lingers today, despite courageous voices to the contrary, including Wesley and Whitefield.

Applying principles of revival and reformation today is most difficult. The reason is that we are no longer enjoying a "Christian consensus," which we were in Europe until 1890 and in America until 1930. Schaeffer's main burden is to prophecy against the decline, in the hopes of strengthening what remains. Beginning at the Enlightenment, a serious weakening occurred, one in which we are still living. Basically, the Enlightenment opened the floodtides for the humanism born at

---

[36] *CW*, 5:127–34.
[37] *CW*, 5:132.
[38] *CW*, 5:135.
[39] *CW*, 5:135–40.
[40] *CW*, 5:141–45.
[41] For further exploration the reader is directed to several volumes. John Piper, *Bloodlines: Race, the Cross, and the Christian* (Wheaton, IL: Crossway, 2011); Carl F. Ellis Jr., *Free at Last? The Gospel in the African-American Experience* (Downers Grove, IL: InterVarsity, 1996); William Julius Wilson, *Bridge over the Racial Divide: Rising Inequality and Coalition Politics* (Berkeley, CA: University of California Press, 1999); John Perkins, *With Justice for All: A Strategy for Community Development*, 3rd ed. (Ventura, CA: Regal, 2007).

the Renaissance.[42] As he does in several of his works, in *How Should We Then Live?*, using rapid-fire prose, Schaeffer covers the French Revolution, the rise of modern science, and then the "breakdown" in all the disciplines. We arrive at modernity, wherein the split between the "upper story" and the "lower story" is established across the board. Whereas the Reformation worldview began to establish the lordship of Christ over every area of life, now we move into the opposite, modern worldview, which places all matters of faith "upstairs" and the rest "downstairs," where things are autonomous.

What are the chief results of this decline? In summary, it would be the loss of absolutes. When there is no longer an "infinite reference point," then the "particulars" are unable to provide meaning.[43] Schaeffer reckons that non-Christian philosophers from the Greeks until just before modernity held three things in common: rationalism, a respect for rationality, and optimism.[44] It is not certain where he derives this interpretation of the history of philosophy. Van Til faults him for not recognizing the perpetual dialectic of rationalist/irrationalist thinking in every age.[45] There have been pessimists from the Greeks onward. And surely Schaeffer knew this. Probably we should think in somewhat relative terms: compared with the ancients, the moderns are particularly prone to irrationalism and pessimism, he might say. Nietzsche is darker than the Stoics, for example. At any rate, Schaeffer looks at previous times, before the line of despair, as somehow closer to biblical norms than are modern times. It occurs to me that he may be describing the shift from what we might call the modernist world to the postmodern condition.[46]

Four crucial areas are affected by the breakdown. While there are more names and dates in *How Should We Then Live?* than in his earlier works, such as *The God Who Is There*, and the outlines change slightly, the basic outlook is the same throughout his works:

1. The first instance of breakdown is within philosophy. After the line of despair, philosophy becomes suspicious of reason and is pessimistic.

---

[42] CW, 5:148.
[43] CW, 5:166, 173.
[44] CW, 5:166–67.
[45] Cornelius Van Til, "The Apologetic Methodology of Francis Schaeffer," March 22, 1974 (on deposit, Montgomery Library, Westminster Theological Seminary, Philadelphia), 39ff.
[46] As far as I know he never engaged in considerations of the modern and the postmodern. Yet his constant plea for rationality (as opposed to rationalism) and his ongoing critique of relativism put him in the same arena as those who would be interacting with postmodernism in later decades. Students who read Schaeffer today are often astonished at how relevant he is to issues such as the postmodern condition.

The chief thinkers leading the way are Rousseau, Kant, Hegel, and Kier-kegaard.[47] Close upon the heals of philosophy is science. During the breakdown, modern science becomes "modern-modern science." Modern science was able to operate because it held to the uniformity of natu-ral causes within an open system, that is, where God was in charge. Eventually, God became the God of the gaps, filling in only when some natural phenomenon was otherwise inexplicable. He became smaller and smaller until eventually he was not needed at all. With Darwin, then neo-Darwinism, the cause-and-effect world was closed and everything became autonomous. Social Darwinism produced the Nazis.[48]

2. Following philosophy and science is the introduction of the "exis-tential methodology." Jean-Paul Sartre and Albert Camus are mentioned. But Martin Heidegger and Karl Jaspers come in for particular attention.[49] Heidegger (1889–1976) begins from the idea of *angst* before the terrible reality of the universe. Yet we may find comfort in the ultimate accessi-bility of being by listening to the poets.[50] Jaspers (1883–1969) similarly speaks of alienation, but then proclaims that there is a way out of the absurd world through having a "final experience."[51] Schaeffer goes on to list the many advocates of such an existentialist approach, from Aldous Huxley, author of *Brave New World*, to rock stars with their hallucinogenic drugs, including Cream, Jefferson Airplane, the Grateful Dead, and Jimi Hendrix.[52] And, tellingly, theology itself follows, moving from the ratio-nalism of Albert Schweitzer to the pessimism of Paul Tillich.[53] Karl Barth in effect practiced the existential methodology, since he advocated faith despite all of the errors in the Bible.

3. Next comes the shift Schaeffer often described in the arts, includ-ing painting, music, literature, and film. Here, he adds the term "frag-mentation" to pessimism.[54] In typical fashion, he reckons that after philosophy, then the arts cross over the line of despair. Such a claim is hard to verify. Did Kant and Hegel come before David and Delacroix? And if so, did these artists read philosophy? They certainly breathed the same air

[47] *CW*, 5:172. It is not certain why Schaeffer did not follow the more standard identification of the "mas-ters of suspicion." For a good introduction, see Merold Westphal, *Suspicion and Faith: The Religious Uses of Modern Atheism* (New York: Fordham University Press, 1998).
[48] *CW*, 5:170–71.
[49] *CW*, 5:184.
[50] *CW*, 5:187.
[51] *CW*, 5:184.
[52] *CW*, 5:186.
[53] *CW*, 5:190–93.
[54] *CW*, 1:27ff.; 5:195ff.

(*Zeitgeist*). Although Schaeffer is no professional art historian and does not engage in the detailed, systematic work of his friend and colleague Hans Rookmaaker, whose *Modern Art and the Death of a Culture* (1973) won him such acclaim, he does exhibit an unusual degree of depth and familiarity when treating the arts, particularly the visual arts. In *How Should We Then Live?* he walks us through the Impressionists, the Postimpressionists, Picasso, Dali, Arp, Duchamp, Pollock, and so many others who represented the shift from unity to fragmentation. The same goes for musicians such as Mahler, Schoenberg, Debussy, and others. Film follows the same trajectory, all markedly declinist, of course. There is none of the nuance here noted by aesthetics scholars in the Reformed movement, such as Calvin Seerveld, with his "Modern Art and the Birth of a Culture."[55] Still, much of it is bold and consistent with Schaeffer view of history.

4. Finally, Schaeffer describes the breakdown in the contours of society. All told, he spends far more time on this category than the others. Many facets emerge. One is his concern for the ideal of personal peace and affluence, so pervasive in middle-class culture. In view of such an essentially bourgeois view of life, young people rebel and look for meaning in places other than the Christian faith. Schaeffer lists the many colorful gurus of the 1960s—Alan Watts, Timothy Leary, Allen Ginsberg, Herbert Marcuse, and others—as prophets of the new way of life based on the utopian dream of dropping out and turning on.[56] Schaeffer worries most about social engineering. Francis Crick, along with a host of scientists, wants something like a complete behavioral control over human beings.[57] Schaeffer's warnings, particularly in *How Should We Then Live?* (the book and the film) convey a distinctly Cold War ambience, as mentioned in chapter 1 of this volume. The same is true for one of his final books, *A Christian Manifesto*.

The most detailed description of the breakdown in society is found in *Whatever Happened to the Human Race?* Coauthored by C. Everett Koop, soon-to-be surgeon general under President Reagan, the book and the film present a host of data, court cases, and anecdotes signaling major threats to human life. Among the issues the authors focus on are genetic manipulation, abortion on demand, child abuse, partial-birth abortion, embryo wastage, infanticide, and euthanasia. Cases and opinions are carefully documented. Behind them, however, is the shifting view of

---

[55] In Calvin Seerveld, *Rainbows for the Fallen World* (Toronto: Tuppence, 1980), 156–201.
[56] *CW*, 1:35ff.; 2:23ff.; 5:211ff.
[57] *CW*, 5:231–44.

human life and the changing approach to legislation that often justifies the unjustifiable.

The shift is from mankind as God's image bearer, and therefore of innate worth, to human beings who are useful. Joseph Fletcher, of *Situation Ethics* fame, describes legitimate life as "meaningful humanhood," and H. Tristram Engelhardt differentiates between "rightful life" and "wrongful life."[58] When people lose their value as people, then substitute definitions arise that measure their worth on any basis besides their ontological constitution. Courts, in order to support this shift, move from interpreting the law to defining it (judicial advocacy). Now that the camel's head is under the tent, there is no reason we could not have another holocaust.[59]

## Hope?

A casual acquaintance with Francis Schaeffer's work might lead to the impression that he was a prophet of doom. If one could weigh up the themes, surely diagnosis would far exceed solutions. And some of it is frankly alarmist. For example, in *Back to Freedom and Dignity*, alongside legitimate causes for worry in various trends, he cites a number of rather zany proposals, including Dr. Kenneth Clark's call for "psychotechnological medication," such as pills that will put an end to international aggression.[60] One should note, at the same time, that Schaeffer is in good company. He surely knew the works of C. S. Lewis, particularly *The Abolition of Man* and *That Hideous Strength*, which have a similar emphasis on the catastrophes wrought in modern history because of the loss of a philosophical view that might undergird human freedom and dignity. And while one could wish for more, there is plenty of hope throughout his writings and speeches. In *A Christian Manifesto*, perhaps his most pessimistic book, still, as mentioned, he describes the 1980 election (the "Reagan Revolution") as a window of hope. He sincerely hoped not only that the abortion ruling would be nullified, but also that negative views could be rolled back "across all of life."[61] Surely, had he lived longer, he would have been discouraged by the lack of progress following this open window.

While not fully Kuyperian, as said before, Schaeffer certainly recognized the need for every portion of life to be redeemed. The fullest

---

[58] *CW*, 5:322–23.
[59] *CW*, 5:340ff.
[60] *CW*, 1:372.
[61] *CW*, 5:457.

statement of possible Kuyperian sympathies I could find is in *Pollution and the Death of Man*. While making the point that Christians have not consistently acted as Christians in regard to the care of God's creation, he shows the difference between animism, with its respect for nature, and the biblical worldview, which respects nature because it is created by God. He illustrates with Abraham Kuyper.

> This [Christian respect for nature] is an extension of Abraham Kuyper's sphere concept. He saw each of us as many men: the man in the state, the man who is the employer, the man who is the father, the elder in the church, the professor at the university—each of these in a different sphere. But even though they are in different spheres at different times, Christians are to act like Christians *in each of the spheres*. The man is *always* there and he is always a Christian under the norms of Scripture, whether in the classroom or at home.
>
> Now, here is the extension: I am a Christian, but not only a Christian. I am also the creature, the one who has been created; the one who is not autonomous, dealing with these other things that equally are not autonomous. As a Christian, I am consciously to deal with every other created thing with integrity, each thing in *its proper sphere* by creation.[62]

To translate: while there is a proper dominion of human beings over nature, in one respect we are dealing with equals. Both humans and the natural world are created and have value as creatures.

Some of Schaeffer's hopeful answers are left in general terms, while some go into detail. If a person becomes a Christian, what should he or she then do? The general advice given in *The God Who Is There* is fourfold: (1) study the Bible, (2) pray regularly, (3) witness, and (4) attend a Bible-believing church.[63] As we have seen, he also speaks to specific spheres of life in his writings and lectures.

### Family

Schaeffer has a number of things to say about family life, some of which we have covered. Spouses should expect not perfection, but true and honest communication.[64] While married people have a right to sexual enjoyment, they have no right to treat their partner as a sex object. Rather, their

---

[62] *CW*, 5:35.
[63] *CW*, 1:148.
[64] *CW*, 3:288.

partner is a human being who needs to be loved.[65] In general, Edith wrote far more about family life than did Fran. Her best-known book on the subject is *What Is a Family?* (1997).

## Business

What about a Christian in business? We have already discussed the notion of a compassionate use of wealth. Schaeffer does not go deep into business ethics, but he does discuss the need to limit the profit motive in order to fulfill the divine command to love one's neighbor. He cites Old Testament legislation to the effect that if you take a man's cloak as collateral, be sure to return it to him on cold nights (Ex. 22:26). While he accepts the idea of private property rights, he defines it to preclude treating one's neighbor as a machine or a "consumer object."[66]

## The Arts

Schaeffer has a bit more to say about being a Christian in the arts. How does the work of a Christian artist reflect his or her faith? First, he argues that a person's style should be contemporary, just as spoken language should be contemporary.

Second, one's style will be appropriate to one's own culture: "If a Christian artist is Japanese, his paintings should be Japanese; if Indian, Indian." Schaeffer was advancing these notions during the rise of consciousness about the relation of art and aesthetics to anthropology. In parallel fashion, the discipline of ethnomusicology was becoming established. There are complex reasons for the growth of these disciplines, including postcolonialism and the reactions to Kant's strictly deontological ethics and to Eurocentrism. Christians, while slow to get on board these more ethnically characterized approaches, began to see the connection of anthropology to missions, the arts, and cultural analysis. For example, ethnomusicology, which stresses the special characteristics of each culture, made Christians aware of ways to feature music for worship and other purposes that draws on local tradition, rather than simply imitating the hymns of the sending country. While not fully engaged with this kind of scholarship, Schaeffer is remarkably prescient about the contextualization in the arts.

---

[65] *CW*, 5:51.
[66] *CW*, 5:51–52.

Third, the body of a Christian's work should reflect a biblical world-view.[67] When Schaeffer elaborates on this, we are not given many specific examples, yet we receive wise counsel on how to express the entirety of a Christian worldview in one's creative output.[68]

## The Sciences

What about a Christian in the sciences? While there are not many specif-ics, Schaeffer shows awareness of the stakes involved in various move-ments and individuals. For example, he generally praises the attitude of Francis Bacon (1561–1626), who advocated searching far and deep not only in the "book of God's word" but also in the "book of God's works."[69] Schaeffer urges scientists to examine their presuppositions and then act as healing agents. For instance, in *Pollution and the Death of Man* he tries to answer critics such as Lynn White, who maintain that the present eco-logical crisis is caused by the "Christian" view of nature as merely the servant of human beings.[70] Instead, Schaeffer wants Christians to revisit their theology and put into practice the call to heal nature from the ill effects of the fall.

One image that is useful in this calling is the church as a "pilot plant."[71] That is, Christians should demonstrate in practical ways how exactly we may have proper dominion over nature without being destruc-tive. They should practice the opposite of England's "Black Country" in the Midlands, where greedy strip miners neglected to restore the topsoil after doing their work. Though it might take a while and yield fewer profits at first, Christian miners should replace the topsoil so that years later a forest can grow, instead of a black desert.[72] They should also practice the oppo-site of the remote Swiss village that lives without electricity for thousands of years, and then suddenly wanting to be powered, doesn't think to bury the ugly wires underground because the process can be hastened with the wires overhead.[73] Schaeffer does not enter into any detailed view of the ecosystem or of the biochemical factors in pollution. He is more attuned to aesthetics than physical danger.

---

[67] CW, 2:405.
[68] Many of us remember the arts festivals at L'Abri, which celebrated painting, poetry, music—all meant to exhibit a Christian sensibility.
[69] CW, 5:362.
[70] CW, 5:66.
[71] CW, 5:47.
[72] CW, 5:48.
[73] CW, 5:49.

### Politics

Finally, what about a Christian in politics? Again, there are many generalities and a few specifics. As already mentioned, Schaeffer discusses the need for a society to be law-based because God is the great Lawgiver. In the absence of such a foundation, the door is open to tyranny. Again, he mentions the genius of checks and balances, based on a realistic understanding of human anthropology.

More controversially, he argues that there will occasionally be the need for a Christian to resist tyrannical government. Schaeffer's most elaborate treatment of church and state issues, *A Christian Manifesto*, is also one of his most controversial. He diligently tries to distinguish between force and violence. There may be legitimate as well as illegitimate uses of force. Without force no legitimate authority or discipline can exist. Violence, however, is excessive force and is never justified. Thus, Schaeffer considers the American Revolution to have been a legitimate use of force against a tyrant. It was not a classical revolution, such as the French or Russian Revolutions, but a "conservative counter-revolution."[74]

On a lesser level, nonviolent use of force might include refusal to pay a portion of one's taxes, or a private school's resisting the Internal Revenue Service encroaching on its affairs. It could include standing in a picket line in front of an abortion clinic.[75] This use of force can be subject to a court trial, but Schaeffer reckons that is part of the cost, as well as a possible opportunity to get a hearing. Because of the fairly emotional tone of the *Manifesto*, I found it difficult to gather exactly which situations require certain kinds of force, and which situations do not.

Again, we do not have here a systematic call to go into politics and work on such things as trade legislation or transportation issues. While Schaeffer does advocate building society up rather than tearing it down, the tone of *A Christian Manifesto* is more along the lines of Bob Dylan's song lyric, which Schaeffer quotes, "When you gonna wake up and strengthen the things that remain?"[76] Because he is a prophet, not a social analyst, Schaeffer's material borders on the alarmist. For example, in chapter 6, he quotes the lawyer Robert Toms, who lists many of the issues pending adjudication during the coming decade. There are thirty-one of them, and

---

[74] *CW*, 5:490.
[75] *CW*, 5:477–78, 484.
[76] *CW*, 5:476.

most are things like prayer in schools, forcing Christian groups to hire people regardless of their lifestyles, posting the Ten Commandments in public, and so on. For me, these are mostly of one kind, relating to church-state border disputes. A number of these are more complicated than Mr. Toms's list implies (his answers are implicitly conservative, if not libertarian). The way they are listed seems almost conspiratorial. Why not list other matters, such as fair trade, peacekeeping abroad, ecology, conservation, community standards, and race matters?

To be fair, Schaeffer does touch on those things from time to time elsewhere. Also, the somewhat alarmist approach to describing cultural strategies is not new here. In the end, he is the carping prophet. His larger issue is the defense of humanity. This is his plea: "We implore those of you who are Christians to exert all your influence to fight against the increasing loss of humanness—through legislation, social action, and other means at your disposal, both privately and publicly, individually and collectively, in all areas of your lives."[77] So, where he might be lacking in a detailed argument for cultural transformation, his approach is hardly devoid of pleas for human rights, beauty, and a healthy relationship between people and their government.

The reader may be wondering what all of this has to do with Christian spirituality. In Schaeffer's mind, a great deal. For one thing, he would never want a human being to be divided into a spiritual and a secular self. To walk with God, to cultivate "reality," can be practiced in one's "prayer closet," but also in the surrounding culture.

A number of years ago, McKendree Langley wrote an important book on Abraham Kuyper, titled *The Practice of Political Spirituality*.[78] This title well expresses how Francis Schaeffer viewed public life. For him all of life, including politics, was a matter of spirituality, just as were prayer life, Bible reading, and the like. Not that he confused the church and the state, as we have seen. Nor that church life should be ignored, or that doing politics, writing a poem, making a scientific discovery, raising a family, and so on are strictly the same kinds of activities. Yet in a deep sense, they are spiritual activities. For Schaeffer, then, spirituality was not restricted to the special practices we often associate with religious devotion.

Here we can emulate the Schaeffers' approach, without necessarily

---

[77] CW, 5:408.
[78] McKendree R. Langley, *The Practice of Political Spirituality: Episodes from the Public Career of Abraham Kuyper, 1879–1918* (Toronto: Paideia, 1984).

living exactly as they did. The work of L'Abri may not be absolutely unique, but such a community—with its approach to prayer, to holding seminars, to discussing major issues around the meal table—is a special model for engaging culture. Other models might look different, though they are no less valid. I know of seminaries and churches that have culture and vocation programs, and of other para-church works that are focused on a particular realm of life, such as science, politics, or the arts. What we should take away from the Schaeffers' teaching and example, and indeed, from the ongoing work of L'Abri around the world, is that Christ is Lord of all of life, and because of that, there is no realm of life not subject to our scrutiny and to our calling as Christians in the world. For many, this message and this practice represent what is so wonderful, so exciting, about the Schaeffer legacy.

# AFTERWORD

## CONCLUDING REFLECTIONS
## ON FRANCIS SCHAEFFER

*Nevertheless, what he said was arresting, however he might look or sound while saying it. It had firmness, arguing vision; gentleness, arguing strength; simple clarity, arguing mental mastery; and compassion, arguing an honest and good heart.*

J. I. PACKER

Having explored a good deal of material from Francis A. Schaeffer's thoughts, particularly concerning spirituality, how do we conclude? What is his legacy? First, I should state clearly that Fran loved his family. He passionately loved his wife. One need only look at some of the interviews he and Edith did together to sense the love between them, whether in open statements or merely the affectionate glances across the way. Like many husbands, he could fuss at her, but it was over silly things, like her pausing too often to pick flowers on a walk or staying up too late before the last bowl of Cheerios! They could also have deeper disagreements, of course. But they were very much in love. And Fran loved his children and grandchildren; it was fun to watch him playing around with them at various reunions. Of course, as we have seen, children were the focus of much of the Schaeffers' ministry. They loved all children!

Second, he was passionate about serving the Lord. Francis Schaeffer left us both an intellectual heritage and an extraordinary example of Christian service. In a way, these go together. He was not one person writing the books and another in personal conversation. They fed upon one another. Os Guinness catches the gist of it with his statement, mentioned in the preface, written in response to Frank Schaeffer's *Crazy for God*:

> One thing above all I will never deny, and for that I am eternally grateful, however great his flaws and however wrong he was on certain details of philosophy and history: *I have never met anyone anywhere like Francis Schaeffer, who took God so passionately seriously, people so passionately seriously, and truth so passionately seriously.* The combination was dynamite, and it is that vision and style of faith, rather than the content of his thinking, which is the debt I owe to him. With Nietzsche, Schaeffer could well have said, "All truth is bloody truth to me."[1]

Taking God, people, and truth "passionately seriously" is what Francis Schaeffer was all about. Why "bloody truth"? Nietzsche's famous *blutige Wahrheiten* means that truth is not aloof from life, but comes at the price of great suffering. Schaeffer's discoveries were almost always the fruit of toils and snares.

Third, one of Schaeffer's most enduring contributions was no doubt to show people, disaffected evangelicals and others, that cultural interests and pursuits are not only legitimate, but part and parcel of being made after God's image and of belonging to his world. For him the arts served a number of purposes. The chief was to illustrate trends and ideas. Even a superficial navigation through his writings and lectures will uncover many illustrations of his thoughts. Beyond that, we occasionally get glimpses of Fran's plain enjoyment of beautiful things and lovely objects. While he did not engage with the deeper issues of aesthetics and artistic issues in technical, philosophical ways, as his friend Hans Rookmaaker did, his work was so full of examples from the arts and other parts of culture that it is clear he reveled in the world of humanity and its way of life, including the beautiful.

Fourth, another most significant contribution made by this Alpine apologist was his uncanny ability to look deeply into a person's heart, uncovering secret aspirations and frustrations. As God's image bearers, every human being is caught in the tension between the sinful assessment of the world and the deep-seated knowledge that God really is there (Rom. 1:20). Schaeffer could bring these tensions to light, all for the sake of giving his interlocutor the good news, the gospel of Jesus Christ. Better,

---

[1] Os Guinness, "Fathers and Sons," *Books and Culture* 14, no. 2 (March/April 2008): 33.

I think, than his great teacher, Cornelius Van Til, Schaeffer could carry out the principles of presuppositional apologetics in actual practice with just about anyone who cared to listen.

Fifth, Francis Schaeffer's greatest spiritual rediscovery was of the present value of the blood of Christ. Some readers may be repulsed or offended by talk of the blood of Christ. The first time I heard the William Cowper hymn about "a fountain filled with blood," all I could think of was a bad Dracula movie. I now realize that the shedding of blood is a profoundly biblical image about the giving up of life for the sake of another. In Jesus's case, his bloody death on Calvary's cross was the fulfillment of all those Old Testament episodes about the sacrifice of goats and bulls, in view of the redemption of God's people (1 Cor. 11:25; Eph. 1:7; Heb. 9:14; etc.). Schaeffer came to realize the present value of Jesus's shed blood in a way that changed everything for him and, as he would claim, led to L'Abri. In a word, it was all about *reality*. This rediscovery was also a window into his better understanding of himself and of "The Movement" he had come from. His constant plea for *reality* was addressed to an evangelical church that had too often lost its vital relationship with God and thus could no longer be the best witness "before the watching world." Indeed, Schaeffer's own reality left a great mark on all who knew him.

Finally, Francis Schaeffer was indeed passionate about people in an unusual way. He cared very deeply about human beings. He particularly reached out to the suffering and confused people of his day. When he preached that there were "no little people," he really meant it. I remember a dinner-table conversation where a very shy young woman wanted to ask a question. She was sure it was not intelligent enough and barely managed to sputter it out. Fran responded, with great sincerity, that he would have to think about it, for it was the most profound question he had heard in years. How she was honored by this response! The incident somehow reminded me of Jesus's defense of the woman who anointed his feet with perfume, declaring before the stuck-up religious leaders at table that she had done a "beautiful thing" (Mark 14:1–11).

I will never forget his reaching out to me—not poor, certainly, but very lost and very *little* spiritually. Thousands of people will agree with me. One of the most moving testimonies of this kind of love is Jerram Barrs's account of Fran's reaching out to Barrs's father in the last days of his life. A hardened Marxist, Jerram's father was nevertheless deeply moved, and

Afterword

eventually led to faith, by the tender care of Francis Schaeffer. While talk about weeping over humanity is cheap, Fran actually did weep over people in their lostness. Occasionally in his films, he actually broke down with tears. Theater? Melodrama? No, this was real. He somehow could suffer along with those who are suffering. Donald Drew alluded to this when asked at a L'Abri conference, "Is there one thing you'd say you've learned at L'Abri?" He thought for a moment, then answered, "I've learned to cry."[2]

Francis Schaeffer had warts, as anyone does. His were at times more visible than those of others, simply because he did so much in public. That he could experience occasional depression is no secret, since he has described some of those bouts himself. Especially when he was tired, he could display a short temper. At times he could sound arrogant, referring to his own writings and to impressive people and places he had influenced. Perhaps he was more vain than arrogant. None of these shortcomings sets him particularly apart from other great leaders, or, indeed, ordinary people. He was human, very human, in the worst way and the very best way!

Perhaps the sermon "No Little People, No Little Places" ironically applied particularly to himself. Small in stature, Francis Schaeffer became a spiritual giant. And while geographically tiny, the village of Huémoz, in the modest country of Switzerland, has been the center for a work, the work of L'Abri, whose impact around the world has been incomparable. Truly, Francis Schaeffer's life was authentic, and his legacy will long endure. He was no little person.

---

[2] Thom Notaro, e-mail message to author, October 15, 2012.

# APPENDIX

## TITLES IN *THE COMPLETE WORKS OF FRANCIS A. SCHAEFFER*

**Volume 1**

*The God Who Is There*

*Escape from Reason*

*He Is There and He Is Not Silent*

*Back to Freedom and Dignity*

**Volume 2**

*Genesis in Space and Time*

*No Final Conflict*

*Joshua and the Flow of Biblical History*

*Basic Bible Studies*

*Art and the Bible*

**Volume 3**

*No Little People*

*True Spirituality*

*The New Super-Spirituality*

*Two Contents, Two Realities*

**Volume 4**

*The Church at the End of the Twentieth Century*

*The Church before the Watching World*

*The Mark of the Christian*

*Death in the City*

*The Great Evangelical Disaster*

**Volume 5**

*Pollution and the Death of Man*

*How Should We Then Live? The Rise and Decline of Western Thought and Culture*

*Whatever Happened to the Human Race?*

*A Christian Manifesto*

# GENERAL INDEX

# SCRIPTURE INDEX

# GAINING WISDOM FROM THE PAST FOR LIFE IN THE PRESENT

*Other volumes in the Theologians on the Christian Life series*

Now Available

June 2013

August 2013

Visit crossway.org for more information.